Simple Mercies

SIMPLE
Mercies

How the Works of
Mercy Bring Peace
and Fulfillment

LARA C. PATANGAN

OSV

Our Sunday Visitor
Huntington, Indiana

Our Sunday Visitor Publishing Division
Our Sunday Visitor, Inc.
200 Noll Plaza
Huntington, IN 46750
www.osv.com
1-800-348-2440

ISBN: 978-1-68192-453-3 (Inventory No. T2337)
1. RELIGION—Christian Life—Women's Issues.
2. RELIGION—Christian Life—General.
3. RELIGION—Christianity—Catholic.

eISBN: 978-1-68192-454-0
LCCN: 2021931457

Cover design/Interior design: Amanda Falk
Cover art: AdobeStock

PRINTED IN THE UNITED STATES OF AMERICA

To everyone who believed I could.
To Helena who insisted I must.
To my husband, Pat, who stands by me come what may.
And, most especially, to Patrick and Alex, so they always
remember they can.

Contents

Contents

Introduction

When my children were young, as routine as saying my nightly prayers, I would recount all the mistakes I had made with them that day. Some failings felt so significant that I would measure them in how many extra years of therapy they would require. While most people worry about saving for retirement, I worried about saving for my children's counseling copays when they were grown and their mama-messed-me-up issues would manifest like a scary clown face popping out of a jack-in-the-box. Now that my boys are in their teens, I look back on those years and the litany of suffering I subjected myself to, and I realize how little I knew God. I couldn't show myself any mercy because I had yet to know his. God was this perfect being who couldn't possibly understand the trials of being an imperfect parent. He had never wrestled anyone with an arched back into a car seat or seen the need to abandon the baby's stroller in the parking lot after realizing it was more likely that *he* would

9

collapse from frustration than the too-complicated-to-fold buggy. Of course, Jesus did wrestle demons, and I am sure collapsing was a possibility when he endured forty days without food or water in the desert. Still, in those early days of motherhood, I relied more on parenting books than our perfect Father.

We live in a world that wants us to do more, have more, be more, and achieve more. Yet falling into this trap of the chase only leaves us with more emptiness. That's how I felt as I was approaching my fortieth birthday: *empty.* I had everything the chase promised except fulfillment, purpose, and peace. So, in many ways I had nothing at all. I was an expert on the *more* the world hawked. But what does God want for me? What does he promise? God's calling is different than the world's. God promises his mercy. I decided to learn more about what that meant, and beginning on my fortieth birthday, I gifted myself with a year of service. By doing corporal and spiritual works of mercy, I came to understand that what I need — what the world needs — is *mercy,* not *more.*

For most of my life, mercy felt above me, like something I could never reach. It was like the incense used during holy days that rose to meet the cherubs at the tops of cathedrals. It was an enigma. I never took the time to contemplate what it meant, how it's shown, or its source from which salvation hinges. Now I understand that mercy never rose to the spires of churches; it descended from the heavens, reaching down to each of us. Mercy is forgiveness, do-overs, compassion, and kindness. I have been on the giving and receiving ends of these things my entire life, but I didn't always recognize them as mercy.

I knew the relief from the burden of sorrow when shown forgiveness. I knew the hope of having another chance. I knew the tenderness of comfort and the warmth of simple kindness. I knew giving these things to others always made me feel better, taught me more about who I am, and had a greater significance than anything on my to-do list. Without mercy, I know I would have no shot at getting into heaven. Mercy is like the golden ticket from *Willy Wonka and the Chocolate Factory*. It gets you access to the most magical place if you choose to redeem it, practice it, and share it.

The corporal works of mercy have to do with how we help our neighbors with their physical needs, and the spiritual works of mercy are ways we meet their spiritual needs. When I began doing works of mercy on my fortieth birthday, I thought that that mercy was something that we do for others, but I quickly realized how desperate I was for its redeeming grace. Knowing God through his mercy has been one of the saving graces of my life. Embracing mercy doesn't mean that we don't suffer; rather, it makes us more aware of the futility of self-imposed suffering. Accepting mercy doesn't mean that we don't acknowledge our mistakes; instead, it allows us to forgive ourselves for them. Mercy isn't about letting anyone off the hook or getting a free pass to do whatever we please; it is a kinder, softer approach to the inherent struggles of our humanity. Practicing mercy is as much a compassionate way of viewing ourselves as it is the way we view others. Understanding mercy allows us to accept the unconditional, perfect love of our heavenly Father, who by his mercy makes us worthy of a love we can't earn on our own.

By making the connection between service and Savior, I discovered that we can transform the mundanity of service into the meaningfulness of worshiping God. Serving doesn't have to be one more thing. It can be *the one thing* that brings us closer to God, fills the empty ache of our humanity, and makes the world a more compassionate, loving place. Saint Faustina acknowledges the importance of the works of mercy in her diary, recording the words she heard Jesus say to her: "Yes, the first Sunday after Easter is the Feast of Mercy, but there must also be deeds of mercy, which are to arise out of love for me. You are to show mercy to our neighbors always and everywhere" (742).

Maybe you've never considered what mercy might look like in your own life before. But if you're looking for fresh, practical ways to live your faith in a meaningful way, consider it now. Like Saint Faustina wrote, consider it "always and everywhere." Hopefully, this book will show you how.

Part One
The Corporal Works of Mercy

1
Feed the Hungry

*"If more of us valued food and cheer and song above
hoarded gold, it would be a merrier world."*

J. R. R. Tolkien

One night I asked my son if he was enjoying the dinner I
cooked. He nonchalantly replied, "I am just trying to eat
it as fast I can, so I don't have to taste it." That epitomizes my
experiences trying to feed people. It's rarely gratifying for me or
satisfying for anyone else. Personally, I can live on popcorn, coffee, and chocolate, so I don't get the big deal about feeding others. I'm just a disastrous cook who once used a serrated knife to
open both a bagged salad and my pointer finger. Without cooking, chopping, or seasoning, I lost a pint of blood, my appetite,

and any latent desire to become the next Julia Child.

Still, the first corporal work of mercy calls us to feed the hungry regardless of our ineptitude. Perhaps this work of mercy is significant because of the universality of hunger. We may not all be foodies, yet we all have to eat. Feeding the hungry addresses more than a rumbling stomach, though. It also seeks to fill the emptiness that gnaws at us. God made us to hunger. And not just for him, but for enriching lives, intimate relationships, and fulfillment of our unique purpose. Everything about you matters to God, even what seems most mundane. A healthy relationship with God considers all aspects of your humanity. Feeding the hungry isn't only about satiating physical hunger by cooking for your family, making your spouse a favorite meal, or feeding the homeless in your community; it also pertains to nourishing your spiritual life and those around you so that you can enjoy a sense of genuine satisfaction regardless of your circumstances. There is a universal hunger that eats at us. This is where a sense of purpose, belonging, and a desire to make a difference originates. And perhaps surprisingly, this hunger in us can be filled through acts of service.

Often, it's the world's sugarcoated lies we consume instead of God's unconditional messages of love and mercy. Although crowded, the world can feel like an empty place. Everyone is running, chasing, or limping along as if they are in some epic battle to cross the finish line. Or, if you're like me, you are just trying not to get run over while mulling which direction to go. Either way, sometimes the journey feels lonely. Meanwhile, the world is bombarding us with gluttonous messages — empty promises sold as ways for us to look good, feel good, or to *finally* be good enough. *Indulge. You deserve it. You earned it. You'll feel better.* Yet, we don't. When I examine my life's trajectory, every steppingstone marked a void to fill. No matter how many times the world had proven me wrong, I still clung to the idea that if I only had *this*, if I could just achieve *that*, then my life would be full. Yet, that's one of the *full of it* messages the world sells. It's the great lie we purchase with our time, money, and energy — the cost of which is calculated not by how much we have but by how empty we feel. This chase of the world's empty promises leaves us constantly craving and always hungry for *more*.

RUNNING ON EMPTY

Sometime in my late twenties, I lamented that I was having a premature midlife crisis. Absurdly, this originated with the Olympic games. I loved watching gymnastics and couldn't help but think that I should be in a leotard flipping and flopping and flying on behalf of my country. Never mind that I had never taken gymnastics in my life. My heart ached to do something with so much passion that it would literally propel me skyward. Plus, I liked the sequins.

At the time, I had a house, some cats, a dog, a good husband, and an inherently meaningful job as a fundraiser for a children's hospital. And yet, I had this nagging feeling that I was meant for *more*. This question of purpose arises intermittently like a bad stomach virus that leaves me longing for the merciful reprieve of a saltine cracker. The search for meaning in my life seems as if it should propel me over obstacles, until I dismount into some profound contribution to humanity, landing with triumph (and yes, maybe even a gold medal). Instead, this quest for meaning throws me off-balance, like a gymnast teetering on the brink of a disastrous fall, leaving me more frustrated than fulfilled. Since my twenties, I have experienced this same desire for purpose multiple times. The great mercy in this search is that I finally realize our contributions to the world aren't always noticeable — even to ourselves.

Recently, a friend who has had a meaningful impact on my spiritual life confided that she feels as if she should be doing something more or different with her life. I understand this emptiness. It's that inherent longing to make a difference, to make our lives count, and to find meaning brilliant enough to shine through the cloud of mundanity that we perceive as life's ordinariness. Yet, no life is ordinary, and your purpose has nothing to do with worldly accomplishments. It is to love and serve God and your neighbor. It is to surrender your expectations and be open and obedient to his.

While desire for purpose is the source of one of the great aches of our hunger, genuine purpose has little to do with what we do and everything to do with how we love. My friend's unwavering trust in God has made my own trust in him grow. As a result of her example, I pray the Rosary daily. I may never see the difference that makes in the world, but I trust that the ripple of what she taught me will spread beyond what either of us will ever see. When I think of that, the question of purpose doesn't seem like it should command so much of the spotlight. It's the answer of love that's the real showstopper. *May you love like you have sequins on.*

JUDGMENT BITES

Like a sugar high followed by a crash, judgment is another source that leaves us empty. Judgments keep us from being open to mercy. For years, my head spiraled with the word *should* as self-judgment dominated the narrative of daily life. You *should* make nicer dinners. You *should* not eat candy. You *should* take that assignment for the newspaper. You *should* volunteer more. You *should* be nicer. You *should* not waste food. You *should* read more. You *should* not complain. You *should* be more organized. You *should* change out of your exercise clothes. You *should* wash your face. You *should* go to confession. You *should* walk the dog. You *should* be more patient. You *should* not have paid that much for a pair of jeans.

These judgments were destructive to my well-being and my relationship with God. Being focused on my inadequacies was a barrier to accepting his love. I understood the merits of God's mercy as they related to others, but I was often unforgiving with myself, skeptical that *he* could really love *me* unconditionally. One of the things I learned from practicing this work of mercy to feed the hungry was that change had to start from within. Being more aware of self-criticism made it easier to recognize the ways judgment sneaked into my interactions with others. Volunteering to feed the hungry

"Let no evil talk come out of your mouths, but only what is useful for building up, as there is need, so that your words may give grace to those who hear."

(Ephesians 4:29)

at the Saint Francis Soup Kitchen reminded me how the sour taste of judgment can spoil our best intentions.

While serving, I noticed a man immersed in conversation, facing away from the baby stroller beside him. Latched inside was a baby reaching toward her father's food. Seemingly oblivious to her hunger, he nonchalantly agreed when I asked to feed her. She ate spoonfuls of chicken and gravy, rice, and carrots. Abruptly, her dad and his friend stood to leave. The baby was still eating, and his indifference to her hunger was maddening. I convinced him to take her uneaten food, hoping she could finish later. Frustrated and on the verge of tears, I wanted that sweet girl to have the same love and attention I strive to give my own kids. No matter how justified I felt, I reminded myself that I wasn't there to judge. I went back to serving hot meals.

I don't know that father's story. I don't know any of the stories of the hundreds of people we fed, or what will become of that little girl or the other children I met. I only know that volunteers serve with respect, recognizing the dignity of all those we serve, the same way Jesus would — without question or judgment. I knew that before I volunteered, but putting it into practice took more effort than serving food, leaving me to wonder if I was doing a work of mercy, or if the real work was what God was doing in me.

THANKFUL

One of the blessings of food is the way it connects us. We don't necessarily think about the sustenance of those connections, about the moments that satiate us in a way that the physical world never will. While Thanksgiving may be the quintessential food holiday, when I revisit memories from my childhood, I am reminded that feeding those we love is about so much more than food. What I recall is the excitement of being out of school for the holiday, the quiet wonder of gazing out the car window at the rows of pines that lined the highway as we traveled to my granny's house, and the creak of the screen door to her modest, two-bedroom home as it flew open, and I rushed inside and straight into her warm and wrinkly arms.

I don't think about the turkey. Instead, I remember running to the park with my siblings and cousins. Using a coveted cardboard box, we perched at the top of a giant hill that spilled onto an oval track. Squeezing together so we would all fit, we flew down the hill on our makeshift sled. We slid easily on the dead grass beneath. The nippy air rushed our faces. My heart raced with a giddy mix of joy and exhilaration. Then, having reached the bottom, we sprinted back up the steep hill to do it again with the same joyful tenacity as a golden retriever fetching a ball. We were tireless despite our pounding hearts, icy hands, and the tattered box that eventually disintegrated into pieces. *I felt free.*

I don't think about how the brown gravy spilled onto my green peas. Instead, I remember curling up next to my Granny and reading from her stack of magazines. I remember the gentle roll of her belly with each inhale and exhale. I folded into her quiet breath and wasn't distracted by the din of the television or the mundanity of adult conversation. *I felt safe.*

I don't think about the punk-red color of cranberry and whether it still had lines from the can that trapped it or the chunky tart texture of my mother's homemade attempt. Instead, I remember my uncle taking us to the Minute Market and handing us each a small brown bag to fill with whatever we wanted. The decadence of his gesture remains a favorite memory. In awe, I carefully picked red-hot fireballs, purple ring-pops, pink bubble-gum cigars, and black envelopes of pop-rocks. *I felt abundance.*

I don't think about the perfectly smooth skin of the brownish-orange pie or the tub of Cool Whip that I much preferred to pie. Instead, I remember giggling when I felt the stubble on my aunt's leg and how when I called them stickers and continuously pet her leg as if she were a porcupine instead of a person, she giggled too. I remember jumping on the sofa bed with my cousins and eventually spilling into the springs that poked me in the back. *I felt peace.*

Thanksgiving isn't about food. It's about gratitude for the people who feed us. That's true of the holiday and our day to day. Cultivating gratitude nourishes us. Being thankful for the time we have with our family that passes too quickly, the moments of joy we steal between all of the rushing and perfecting, and the memories that sustain us after those we love pass on is more satisfying than the heartiest meal. Giving the people in our lives something to be thankful for beyond physical sustenance touches our hearts in a way that years later reminds us how small things become big. With abandon, I glide into gratitude for the people in my life as if I were still a small child huddled on a cardboard box ready to descend, only this time, into a warm memory. For all of it, *I feel thankful.*

FOOD FOR THOUGHT

If you, like me, are mired in the immediate and every day, the thought of adding anything more to your to-do list probably has you reaching for antacids. Yet you were created in the image of God to serve others, which makes feeding the hungry integral to your fulfillment — not an optional extra. Thankfully, integrating works of mercy into your daily life doesn't have to be complicated. Too often I have felt my contributions were too small to make a difference. I can't stop world hunger — much less the hunger in my community — but by donating some extra food, I can become a part of the whole that could. That is empowering.

Thankfully, there are many practical and meaningful ways to incorporate this work of mercy into daily life. The most significant way to feed the hungry is the way Jesus did with the fishes and the loaves. "They replied, 'We have nothing here but five loaves and two fish. And he said, 'Bring them here to me.' Then he ordered the crowds to sit down on the grass. Taking the five loaves and the two fish, he looked up to heaven, and blessed and broke the loaves, and gave them to the disciples, and the disciples gave them to the crowds" (Mt 14:17–19). Jesus made an abundant feast with meager resources, and while we can't multiply fish, we can be part of the exponential power of good deeds.

Serving others is a hallmark of Christian faith and one of the surest ways to fill the void in our lives. There are many ways you can feed the hungry physically. You can volunteer at the local soup kitchen, invite an elderly person over for dinner, carry nonperishable food items in your car to pass out to the homeless, or donate food to the food bank. Bringing a meal to the bereaved or even the simplicity of cooking dinner for your family (even when it's humbling) are also important ways to feed the hungry. Also, being mindful not to waste food is a relatively easy way to do this work. One night for dessert, I bought one chocolate-covered strawberry for each family member. It was perfect and felt decadent to have just enough, instead of always having *more*.

Recognizing that we become agitated and restless when we are dissatisfied with relationships, fail to recognize the meaning of our lives, and are starving for a morsel of mercy to rest and refuel, can help us think creatively about how to feed others spiritually. By cultivating your children's unique talents, you help them grow. You can feed your spouse with love and support and season your friendships with encouragement. Teaching others about the nourishment of God's love is an act of mercy and of evangelization. Whether you are feeding hungry bodies or hungry souls, it's the love behind the act that makes it meaningful. While the world may only applaud our service if it's as fancy as a three-tiered wedding cake, God delights in our small acts of love. He knows both our limits and our potential. It's not about adding to your already full plate. Instead, it's making sure

> *"This is the bread that came down from heaven, not like that which your ancestors ate, and they died. But the one who eats this bread will live forever."*
>
> *(John 6:58)*

that what's on those plates feed your purpose: to love and serve God and your neighbor.

MERCY WORKS: TRY IT

Saint Teresa of Avila said, "Know that even when you are in the kitchen, our Lord moves amidst the pots and pans." Below are some ways you can move your heart closer to God by feeding the hungry.

- *In your home*: It doesn't matter if you are serving leftovers or a gourmet meal, serve with love. Light candles, play music, use wine glasses for water — do something simple to make mealtime special. Involve your children in meal preparation. If your children are old enough, designate someone to be the server each night, and give them the special task of waiting on others. Focus on the conversation and allow your family time to pause from the busyness of the world and reconnect to one another. Surprise your spouse with a picnic. Mealtime is the perfect opportunity to rediscover the bounty of blessings in our lives.

- *In your community*: Organize a food drive at work or at your children's school. Buy groceries for a struggling family. Participate in a bake sale or volunteer at a local soup kitchen. Carry granola bars or other small snacks with you in your car or purse to share with a hungry person you might encounter.

- *In your personal relationship with God*: Make the connection between your love for God and the service of meal planning, cooking, and feeding others.

Offer up the sacrifice involved. Remember Saint Teresa's words (quoted above) amidst the mundanity of feeding your spouse and children, and recognize our Lord's presence in your service. Pray while you wash dishes. Express gratitude for your food. Acknowledge the fullness that only God offers. Attend Mass as often as possible and enjoy the feast of true communion with God.

REFLECTION QUESTIONS

What are you hungry for in your life? What messages make up the majority of your spiritual diet — are they from the world or the word of God? What feeds you and what leaves you aching for more? How can your relationship with God help fill the source of your ache?

In what ways can you feed your spouse and kids words of affirmation in areas where they feel empty? What are some concrete ways you can grow your family's faith life around meals?

How can you "feed" others on a daily basis by imitating Jesus' example of the fishes and the loaves turning small acts into an abundance of love?

PRAY

Dear Heavenly Father, please help me seek you to fill the hunger I feel in my life instead of turning to the world's menu of emptiness for satisfaction. Thank you for the banquet of blessings that you have gifted to me in this world and help me to fixate on the endless bounty that awaits in your heavenly home so that I can someday join you there. Guide me in my service so it reflects the fullness of your love and the abundance of your mercy. Draw me closer to you, my Lord, the true bread of life.

2

Give Drink to the Thirsty

*"The reason for our existence is to quench the
thirst of Jesus. When he asked for water, the
soldier gave him vinegar to drink — but his
thirst was for love, for souls, for you and me."*

Saint Teresa of Calcutta

A television commercial for Calgon, a manufacturer of bath
products, once featured an overstressed woman lament-
ing everything from the barking dog to the screaming kids. On
the verge of a televised breakdown, she pleads, "Calgon, take me
away!" Instantly she appears in a bathtub covered in foaming
bubbles and calm. When I think of the work of mercy to give
drink to the thirsty, I picture those mountains of bubbles float-

ing where a lady once sank. Maybe that seems irrelevant, because this work of mercy is about giving drink, not taking baths. Yet the relief those seemingly magical bubbles offered a frazzled woman reminds me of God's unquenchable mercy, which offers peace long after a twenty-minute soak in the tub.

Like the woman grasping her head and the remnants of her sanity, we too get consumed by the hectic pace of modern life. One morning I woke late, and stumbling to get my coffee, I hit my shin on the bottom drawer in the kitchen that was carelessly left open. Seconds later, while I was getting the milk from the refrigerator, my finger slammed in the freezer door. (Trust me, I know that makes no sense.) Then, I jammed the mascara wand in my eye and all the inky goo, which moments before sat like wet paint on my lashes, smeared my skin in a splatter of black reminiscent of a Jackson Pollock painting. *Can't anyone see how hard I am trying?* I thought. I am not sure who I thought needed to see. Even I couldn't say definitively what I was trying so hard at or for. I just knew that life felt particularly difficult. Small things. Insignificant tasks. To-do lists of my own tyranny. I was thirsting for some sign of recognition and direction from God. *Did he see me? Was any of it his will for my life? Did he command me to color my light lashes dark with a surgeon's precision and a two-inch wand?*

I was scheduling and schlepping with the good intentions of bettering my family, myself, and those I encountered. When you stretch, push, and bend to accommodate life's constant demands, you may not realize how thirsty you are for the respite of God. Sometimes trying so hard becomes more of a distraction and a disservice to our spiritual life than the delineator of his love that we long to be. While every living cell in our bodies needs water to function, we underestimate our physical dependence on it. Similarly, this happens with our relationship with God. Instead of drinking in the blessing of a loving and merciful God, we often push aside what is paramount for what is passing. Giving drink to the thirsty isn't just about your physical needs; relieving your spiritual thirst is also critical to your wellbeing.

Of all the works of mercy, giving drink to the thirsty often seems the most archaic. After all, most of us living in developed countries have ready access to clean drinking water. It freely flows from our faucets, and we often don't give a second thought to our dependence on it. You need water to survive physically in the same way you need God to survive spiritually. Without either, we are dead. You may have fizzy water in the fridge, but life will feel flat if you are caught in the world's current instead of flowing in communion with God. All of the running and chasing that make up a day often leave us thirsty for more than a cold drink. If you are desperate for relief, you are not alone. We live in a thirsty world. The lonely thirst for companionship. The new kid at school thirsts for a friend. Those with carefully crafted facades thirst for authenticity. The grieving thirst for comfort. The homeless thirst for dignity. The abandoned thirst for belonging. The victimized thirst for justice. We thirst for recognition, appreciation, value, intimacy, love, and forgiveness.

> *"O God, you are my God, I seek you; / my soul thirsts for you; / my flesh faints for you, / as in a dry and weary land where there is no water."*
>
> *(Psalm 63:1)*

This work of mercy isn't just about making sure everyone's physical thirst is relieved or that their spiritual needs are met. It also seeks to address the importance of respecting our environment, especially as it pertains to our waterways. Giving drink to the thirsty is integrally tied to our environmental responsibilities. You can make a difference whether it's through recycling, water conservation, or reducing meat consumption. Perhaps the biggest thing you can do is nothing. By forsaking conspicuous consumption, you can have a major impact on the environment. Less production, waste, materialism, debt, and greed allow us to better meet the needs of humanity. Caring for the earth — recognizing it as a gift that is both for our pleasure and sustenance — enables us to give drink to the thirsty.

YOU CAN LEAD A HORSE TO WATER, BUT YOU CAN'T MAKE HIM DRINK

I'm not really going to write about horses. Instead, I'm going to write about cats. Not so secretly, I aspire to be a cat lady. While I have always owned a cat, I have never intentionally adopted one. They just show up. When they do, I tell my husband that God sent them. I figure there is no way he is going to turn down a cat from God because that would not only make his lovely wife mad, but it would disappoint God, too. So far, this strategy has worked for me, God, and the cats. Surprisingly, I once learned a great lesson about the gift of mercy from one of these rescue cats.

The irony of having spent a year of my life focused on doing works of mercy was that when it was over, I ached for the very mercy I chased. I saw so much suffering and sadness that year: an eleven-year-old girl with a relapse of leukemia; a woman anguishing over the child she aborted; an immigrant family who escaped the violence of their native country only to have their father killed in a car accident caused by a wrong-way driver; and what felt like too many other instances of heartbreaking sorrow. Compared to the suffering I encountered, any works of mercy I did never felt like enough. *I* never felt like enough. I believed the world's lie that

I, and my acts of service, needed to be *more* in order to matter. While I was desperate for God's mercy, for the promise of his unconditional love, I thought I had no right to it when other people needed it far worse than I did. I believed I had to earn God's love. I pushed aside my conflict from that year and without realizing it, I shoved God's mercy aside, too. Spiritually dry, I felt untethered. I wasn't sure if I was going to fall or break or merely float away.

During this time, I found two kittens on the side of my house. While both cats were feral, one appeared to be possessed by Satan. She would growl and hiss and make bizarre demonic sounds that seemed unfitting for something so miniature and cute. I shut the kittens in a small bathroom and sat with them for hours with my feet crouched on the toilet seat to avoid demon kitty's attack. Despite being hissed at when I made the slightest move, I spent as much time as possible in confinement with them. Days went by, and I was desperate to tame them. I bought special goats' milk, wet food, and kitty toys. Even though I was terrified of that tiny ball of terror, I kept trying to pet her as well as her more docile sister. Patiently and purposefully, I refused to give up.

> *"But those who drink of the water that I will give them will never be thirsty. The water that I will give will become in them a spring of water gushing up to eternal life." (John 4:14)*

Like that demon kitty ridiculously fighting the one who could save it, I realized I was also resisting the relief of God's mercy.

Whether it's from a sense of unworthiness, busyness, or merely a lack of awareness, we are often unnecessarily parched. God alone offers relief from the agony of your thirst. Those kittens, and perhaps the hours of solitude I spent with them, reminded me that we are never floating in the darkness alone. We are tethered to God, not by our doing, but by his. He will never let you go. He's never going to give you up. Mercy is abundant, but you choose whether or not to take the cup. Once I realized this, the choice was clear. I am never going to resist his mercy just as my now angelic cat never seems to resist being at my side.

SPIRITUAL EVOLUTION

When I was in college, I had a friend who often wore Birkenstocks, the backless shoes that are the tree-hugging cousin of the flip-flop. The shoes reminded me of the Hare Krishna food they gave away on campus and earthy people who touted the merits of granola. This was back in the nineties before Nordstrom carried the comfort shoe in an array of pastels as a luxury brand. I was broke in college, so a splurge for me were the fifty-nine-cent tacos at Taco Bell. It would have been healthier to eat the free food passed out by the bald people wearing white sheets and dancing with tambourines. But I was afraid it would cause me to disavow my beachy flip-flops for their chunkier cousin. I didn't consider myself an environmentalist then. I figured I was doing my part by reusing the same plastic cup at nickel beer night.

As the years passed, I developed an affinity for nature that gave me a broader perspective. I came to realize that care for the environment is an important aspect of giving drink to the thirsty. In an effort to honor that, my family and I spent a day picking up trash along the riverbank. It may not have been giving drink to the thirsty in the literal sense, but it was a way to acknowledge the importance of ready access to clean drinking water by protecting its source. When we finished our trash pickup, we carried our heavy bags like badges of pride. It felt like an offering of penance for the ways we sometimes take for granted the beauty of creation.

Being in nature is one of the few places where I feel completely at peace. There, I have no sense of time, no need for email, no concern about social media, no worries about the future, and no misconceptions about who I am. It's a holy place where I recognize the wonder of God that roots into the unseen earth and stretches skyward with an umbrella of branches. The lessons I learn from nature are as uncomplicated as they are profound. Recognizing this has made the seemingly obscure work of mercy to give drink to the thirsty relevant. I have a better understanding of how it ties in to our environmental responsibilities as Christians.

"For the kingdom of God is not food and drink but righteousness and peace and joy in the Holy Spirit. The one who thus serves Christ is acceptable to God and has human approval."

(Romans 14:17–18)

In 2015, while speaking to a group of young people at Santo Tomas University in Manila, Pope Francis emphasized our Christian responsibility to care for the environment. "A second key area where you are called to make a contribution is in showing concern for the environment. ... You are called to care for creation not only as responsible citizens, but also as followers of Christ!" So much changes with times, trends, and the progression of our opinions, yet honoring nature is every day, ever-evolving, much like that girl I was in college. The one who eventually walked away from the environmentalist stereotypes toward the God who created it all, loves all, and is in all. Now that's something to celebrate whether it's with tambourines or tacos.

WET YOUR WHISTLE (AND WHISTLE WHILE YOU WORK)

While we instinctively thirst for God, this work of mercy isn't only about drinking in the merciful relief he offers; it's also about our call to serve. I like to think the song "Whistle While You Work," from Disney's *Snow White*, is really about works of mercy. It's a perfect reminder of how we can emphasize the joy of doing God's work over the monotony it sometimes involves. Our spiritual thirst can be satisfied through all of those things we do in a day that feel insignificant but are meaningful to God and our neighbor when we do them with the intention of love.

> *"The* LORD *is my shepherd, I shall not want. / He makes me lie down in green pastures; / he leads me beside still waters; / he restores my soul." (Psalm 23:1–3)*

There are many tangible ways we can give drink to the thirsty: nursing a child or pouring them a glass of milk with their dinner; caring for our waterways by picking up trash; appreciating our ready access to clean drinking water and supporting organizations who make it possible for others to have it, too; volunteering to pass out water at a charity run; bringing your spouse a cup of coffee in the morning; carrying water bottles in your car to pass out to homeless people; leaving a bowl of water at your business or in front of your house for thirsty animals; considering water conservation efforts when landscaping; and passing out popsicles to neighborhood kids on a hot day. More than anything, we can give drink to the thirsty by always being ready to pour out mercy on others in our daily lives.

Perhaps Jesus turning water into wine at the wedding in Cana best exemplifies the work of mercy to give drink to the thirsty. Not because everyone prefers Pinot to Perrier, but because it was both an act of reverence toward his blessed mother, Mary, and his first public miracle. Through his mercy, God offers us the same miracle of transformation. Only from God can we experience relief from our burdens, from our past, and from whatever labels the world assigns. Only through his redemptive mercy can we wash away our former selves and become a new creation. The constancy of God's mercy, its abundance, and its power to turn the darkest parts of us into light, is a moment-by-moment miracle that is ours for the taking. Like our blessed Virgin Mother at the wedding at Cana, all we have to do is ask.

MERCY WORKS: TRY IT

Mark Twain wrote, "High and fine literature is wine, and mine is only water; but everybody likes water." While wine is certainly fancier, the power of water to restore, cleanse, and renew is unparalleled. Remembering the unquenchable gift of God's mercy, move your heart closer to God as you give drink to the thirsty.

- *In your home*: Practice water conservation efforts. Use reusable water bottles. Teach your children to turn off the water when they brush their teeth and to only put their clothes in the hamper when they are actually dirty. Share with your family the importance of staying hydrated. Have each member chart their water intake for a week to see how much (or little) they are drinking. Go out for wine with your spouse and enjoy relief from the daily grind. Practice whistling while you work and feel the joy in serving others even in mundane and ordinary ways. Let your family know that, like God's mercy, they can count on one another for forgiveness, renewal, and a fountain of unconditional love.

- *In your community*: Plan an activity that involves giving drink to the thirsty. Volunteer at a charity run to pass out water. Donate water to a homeless shelter or to those affected by natural disasters. Raise money for an organization that provides clean drinking water. Consider those who thirst for something beyond the physical: Give a weary mother a spiritual drink by offering to babysit her kids for a few hours. Treat a friend who is going through a difficult time to coffee. Pay attention to signs of loneliness, indifference, and unsatisfaction in others and remind them of God's unconditional mercy.

- *In your personal relationship with God*: Make the connection between your thirst and the only one who can quench it, our Lord and Savior. Rely on his love and mercy, not on the ways of the world, to offer respite. Take a bubble bath! While its relief is temporary, God wants us to enjoy moments of rest and relaxation. Go to confession and let his mercy wash away the sins of your past so you can begin again. Pray for the renewal of your mind and heart and that of humankind. Drink in the goodness of our Savior and share the good news of his unquenchable mercy with others.

REFLECTION QUESTIONS

How do you recognize your own spiritual thirst and that of your spouse and children?

What conservation efforts can you make in daily life?

How can you show mercy to yourself in a way that frees you to devote more time to your relationship with God?

PRAYER

Dear God, please help me to turn to you for relief and renewal and not to rely on temporary pleasures for fulfillment. Transform my life by washing away my sins, my resistance to your mercy, and all that separates me from you. Help me to be joyful and to drink in the blessings of my life while I care for others and the environment. May the only thirst I know be for your unquenchable love.

3
Clothe the Naked

*"Do not adorn yourselves outwardly by braiding
your hair, and by wearing gold ornaments or fine
clothing; rather, let your adornment be the inner
self with the lasting beauty of a gentle and quiet
spirit, which is very precious in God's sight."*
1 Peter 3:3–4

Sometimes all I see hanging in my closet are dubious choices. Impractical prints that have gone from perfect to puzzling, too snug skirts that mock me, and artful shoes that make me wince in agony — all squished together in a kaleidoscope of wasted time and money. Down to the ultra-thin hangers designed to maximize coveted closet space, we're sold the misconception

39

that our value is intrinsically tied to appearances and posses-sions. From the size of our bodies to the style of our clothes, we're inundated with messages about what's considered accept-able, desirable, and admirable. Fashion magazines portray wisps of women wearing outrageously expensive clothes that look more suitable for a circus performance than the routine of real life. We're pushed products to dissect our bodies into sections to suffocate, and parts to enlarge, leaving our sense of wholeness in pieces. We own enough clothes and yet buy more to cover our inferiority, shame, and inadequacy. The work of mercy to clothe the naked offers the opportunity to reflect beyond appearances in the mirror. It's not just about literal clothing — by performing this work, we will better see ourselves through the unconditional love and mercy of our heavenly Father.

I've wrapped myself in the superficial that society hawks. Yet I know that the joy of buying new things is unsustainable, and nothing like the satisfaction I get from my relationship with God. In our society, most of us own far too many clothes. Certainly, there are people who need help finding clothing, such as a woman fleeing an abusive relationship, families affected by natural disas-ters, parents who can't afford to replace their children's outgrown clothes, and the homeless who lack proper shoes or jackets. But we should also think about clothing the naked on a deeper level. What if it's to clothe the nakedness of our souls with the regal gar-ment of God's love? What if it's to cover those who are suffering from the shame of sin with the redemption of God's mercy? What if it's to armor ourselves in the teachings of Scripture? What if it's to wear the truth of God so that others may know him?

From kindergarten through high school, I wore a uniform. Not until college, when limitless apparel options became la-bored, did I realize the blessing of plaid. Still, in grade school, my classmates and I enjoyed occasional non-uniform days when we paid a quarter for the luxury of wearing street clothes. When

I was in the fourth grade, my mom took me shopping for an upcoming non-uniform day. I found the perfect outfit: purple pants and a floral shirt with dainty sleeves that delicately covered my shoulders with two tiny poufs. In my nine-year-old mind, it was the epitome of 1980s panache. (Only, I am pretty sure I did not know what that word meant.) My mom didn't like the outfit and suggested alternatives, but I *really* liked the purple pants panache. My mother succumbed, and twenty-five cents later I wore my new outfit to school. Clothes in their basic form cover our bodies. They protect us from the elements of sun, rain, and snow. Yet they are more than practicalities. They are a means of self-expression. We all have certain things we are comfortable wearing and others that we wouldn't consider. When we shop, we may say, "It just doesn't look like me." Everyone has a guise that makes them feel comfortable, dignified, and confident.

We are encouraged to clothe the naked because dignified clothing makes people feel worthy. As a child, I often wore hand-me-downs, so getting that new purple outfit was important to me. Clothes give a glimpse of our identity — the executive, athlete, fashionista, hippie, preppie, or *Thomas the Tank Engine* devotee. Few would choose to look poor, wearing ill-fitted pants, stained shirts, ratty shoes, and tattered

> *"I sought the* Lord, *and he answered me / and delivered me from all my fears. / Look to him and be radiant; / so your faces shall never be ashamed."*
>
> *(Psalm 34:4–5)*

jeans that, unlike some expensive pair from a boutique, were not designed to have holes in them. Wearing something nice makes us feel good about ourselves, like we have value. Clothes, in their basic form, are meant to cover our nakedness. They are necessary practicalities. What we wear determines how others see us. While we don't need to get caught up in keeping up, we have an obligation as disciples of Christ to make sure we wear the dignity of our faith, not the dinginess of materialism and vanity. While this includes serving others so that their physical needs are met, it also ensures the spiritual comfort of wearing God's unconditional love and mercy. Clothing the naked offers fulfillment that lasts far longer than an adrenaline-fueled shopping spree.

WOLF IN SHEEP'S CLOTHING

It's easy to fall prey to the world's messages of self-worth and value. It's fun to snag a deal or find a flattering outfit, and there is nothing wrong with looking attractive. It's when we tie our identity to trends or to what hangs in our closet that we become distracted from our ultimate purpose to love and serve God. While we were created in his image, the world tells us it's the image of magazine covers, movie stars, and celebrity icons we should glorify. The majority of advertising messages target ways to look more attractive, fight aging, lose weight, and dress better. The commonality of this quest to look like an airbrushed version of an advertiser's aspiration is our universal desire for love and acceptance. Our vulnerability is exploited when we fixate on buying wrinkle cream, diet pills, and designer clothes instead of seeking fulfillment through our service to God and our neighbor. We are encouraged to open our wallets instead of our hearts, which leaves us spiritually poor and naked. You can armor yourself against these lies with the truth of Scripture. Like Adam and Eve in the garden of Eden, who were shamed by their nakedness, you have a choice between listening to the word of God or the whims of man. One whispers you are enough and the other roars that you never will be.

Sometimes when we sin, shame further separates us from God. Saint John Chrysostom explained it well when he said, "Pay attention carefully. After the sin comes the shame; courage follows repentance. Did you pay attention to what I said? Satan upsets the order; he gives the courage to sin and the shame to repentance." For years, I avoided confession because of this shame of repentance. Humiliated by my imperfections, by all the ways I failed God, I wore the heaviness of sin.

"Do not look on his appearance or on the height of his stature, because I have rejected him; for the LORD does not see as mortals see; they look on the outward appearance, but the LORD looks on the heart."

(1 Samuel 16:7)

My sins were like moths slowly eating away at the garment of my salvation. It was as Saint John warned: Satan had upset the order. Instead of recognizing the cloak of courage worn after absolution, I confused it with shame.

OH, BABY

When I helped pass out baby and maternity clothes at the Women's Help Center (a pro-life organization that encourages doubtful women to see their pregnancy as a blessing, not a burden),

I realized how easily we can make a difference. Before my son was born, I had more diapers in my over-prepared baby arsenal than they had on their shelves. Still, like the parable of the fishes and loaves, we had enough to give to the women who came to us. Sadly, this wasn't the case when one woman was looking for maternity jeans. I felt badly, remembering how hard it is to find anything that fits well when you're pregnant.

Inspired by this organization's mission and the gratitude of the people we served, I asked members of my church's women's circle to join me in hosting a baby shower. Our circle is named after Saint Gianna, the patron saint of mothers. She was a devoted mother, physician, and wife best known for refusing an abortion, despite knowing that continuing the pregnancy could result in her death. Gianna was canonized a saint in 2004, and her last child, the one she sacrificed her life for, attended the canonization. In the spirit of our patron saint, our circle was ever generous, donating everything from maternity clothes to strollers and ensuring the diaper closet was well-stocked. Many of our members still have young children, so they passed along their outgrown clothes. Before, I never considered who I was helping when I donated clothes. Now, seeing the recipients' grateful faces helped me realize how much castoffs can matter. When you want as badly as I did to give a pregnant mother a pair of jeans that fit, you realize that cleaning out your closet truly makes a difference.

PRETTY IN PINK

In home economics class our quarter project was to sew boxer shorts. Excited about the assignment, I picked a fabric with pretty pink flowers on a pink background. It looked vintage and chic. I figured Molly Ringwald would want to borrow my boxer shorts if she did a sequel to *Pretty in Pink*. To my dismay, there was no sequel, and considering how my boxer shorts came out, it was just as well. I cut, poked, and stitched in all the wrong places. I resigned myself to sleeping in old T-shirts for the rest of my life. I barely got a D, which was crushing since the class was home ec., not rocket science.

So when I heard about a nonprofit that involved sewing, I was skeptical. Yet, Rethreaded's mission is beautiful, no matter your sewing skills. According to the Jacksonville-based business's website: "Rethreaded seeks to unravel the effects of the sex trade, whether it takes the form of human trafficking, prostitution, pornography or strip clubs." Women who have experienced addiction, violence, and prostitution are taught self-worth, dignity, and a new way of life by becoming seamstresses. They transform old donated T-shirts clothes, bags, purses, and scarves. The physical transformation of their beautiful, custom-made wares pale in comparison to how they change worn, tired, and broken lives into the vibrant colors of hope. Rethreaded trains women to become artisan seamstresses, pays a living wage, and, most importantly, redresses them with dignity, compassion, and love.

My boys and I spent an afternoon working with them in a warehouse downtown. There were rainbows of worn T-shirts of every size, color, and logo imaginable lining walls, filling bins, and dangling from hangers. We sorted T-shirts by color, following a Pantone chart with names like vivacious, koi, and turbulence. It was stifling hot. Yet it felt cathartic to sweat alongside these women who are brave enough to choose a different pattern for their lives. I explained to my boys that we were helping women who have had a hard life, maybe been on drugs, homeless, or somehow hurt by others. Raising children in an

"Strength and dignity are her clothing, / and she laughs at the time to come." (Proverbs 31:25)

over-sexualized culture, I wanted them to understand the proper context of sex: Within love and marriage, it is a gift. It should never be violent. Nor is it something to sell or give away without regard to its sacred nature. It is a challenging message to convey in a world where sex is a commodity, consent is ignored or given freely, and pleasure takes priority over people. Of course, my boys didn't understand all that at the time. But someday, they'll recall how they sweated alongside their mama, amid the rainbow of T-shirts. They'll understand why what they did was important. They'll know what it means to respect women's bodies and their own. Rethreaded enables women to rediscover the vivid colors unique to their lives, so they can begin to create a new tapestry sewn with love into a timeless story of hope. Maybe these women will title it *Pretty in Pink*. No, that wouldn't quite do. A story like that would have to begin with *Beautiful*.

> *"As God's chosen ones, holy and beloved, clothe yourselves with compassion, kindness, humility, meekness, and patience."*
>
> *(Colossians 3:12)*

ALL DRESSED UP (WITH SOMEPLACE TO GO!)

As Christians, we have the gift of knowing our inherent value as human beings, and this offers us many reasons to rejoice. To know God is to experience the unparalleled joy of belonging to him. We recognize the Good News of the Gospel and what it reveals about our salvation. Regardless of what happens in this world, a heavenly world awaits where there is no sadness, affliction, sin, or death — only the glorious bliss of God. Why wouldn't we dress ourselves in the joy of our Redeemer and proclaim it to the world? It's such happy news.

Works of mercy transcribe service into joy. Clothing the naked is a powerful way we can serve others while sharing the Good News of God's mercy. God isn't concerned with how we look but with how we look to serve others. By donating clothes to a shelter, collecting socks and jackets for the homeless, or buying diapers for babies whose mothers can't afford them, we can adorn ourselves with good works for the Lord. It doesn't have to be complicated. There are many ways to serve.

I once interviewed a hairdresser for a newspaper article, who gave free haircuts to residents of a homeless shelter. One man burst into tears upon seeing himself after she cut his hair. He told her that he looked the way he had remembered himself before becoming homeless. She didn't pass out clothes that day, but by offering her talents, she clothed a man in the dignity that his circumstances had stripped from him. Likewise, we can be fashionistas for God by wearing our hearts on our sleeve as we serve others.

MERCY WORKS: TRY IT

Saint Elizabeth of Hungary asked, "How could I wear a crown of gold when my Lord wears a crown of thorns and he wears it for me?" Knowing Christ suffered for our salvation, we can joyfully clothe others in the dignity and love of his redemption. Here are some ways you can practice clothing the naked.

- *In your home*: Clean out closets and donate excess clothes to the poor. Shop from your closet (and your friends' closets!). Create new outfits by using accessories and pairing together different items you already own. Encourage your children to get involved by adopting a family at Christmas or donating backpacks at the beginning of a school year. Shop at thrift stores and support the good work of charity while snagging a deal. Teach children charity by setting aside a portion of their allowance to purchase diapers, pajamas, socks, and underwear for the needy. Collect hygiene items and toiletries and donate them to your local homeless shelter. Surprise your spouse by ironing their clothes. Teach your children what it means to dress themselves in the dignity of God so that others may know what it means to be clothed in his love.

- *In your community*: Organize a clothing drive at your place of work, church, or any clubs you belong to. Volunteer to distribute clothes to the needy so you experience how much your generosity matters. Support businesses that are fair-trade certified or made in the United States to ensure you are not unknowingly exploiting child or slave labor. Refuse to contribute to the world's shaming messages by refraining from judgment. Instead, proclaim the joy of Christ's love so that others may experience it too.

- *In your personal relationship with God*: Make a daily effort to clothe yourself with the word of God so the world's messages of shame cannot influence you. Meditate on what it means to be clad in the dignity of Christ. Prayerfully consider the words of Saint Anthony of Padua, who said, "Nowhere other than looking at himself in the mirror of the cross can man better understand how much he is worth."

Look at your worth as God does and know that regardless of what you weigh or what you wear, you
are priceless to him.

REFLECTION QUESTIONS
Do you judge people by what they wear or how they look? How
do stereotypes affect your interactions?

How can you balance buying your children clothes that feel like
"them," while also teaching them that our value doesn't come
from what we wear?

What are some ways you can support charities in your community, starting with what's in your closet?

What are some concrete ways you can dress (and address) your
spouse in dignity?

PRAYER
Dear Heavenly Father, help me strip away the message of the
world that says my value is tied to my appearance, so that I may
remember my true worth comes from you. You deemed me precious when you died on the cross for my salvation. Help me to
be joyful in this truth, to clothe myself in good works, and not to
concern myself with the reflection in the mirror, but with the way
I reflect your love to my neighbor. Help me to be mindful of the
ways I can cover others in compassion, justice, and dignity. Amen.

4
Shelter the Homeless

"It is in the shelter of each other that the people live."

Irish proverb

Life can feel like the tornado in *The Wonderful Wizard of Oz* — a daily twister of to-dos, tasks, and relentless trying. We try to be good people, exemplary parents, and invaluable employees. We try to be healthy, keep up with laundry, and floss our teeth. We try to return emails, plan family vacations, and remember to pick the kids up from practice. Often left dizzy from all this striving, you may not see how desperate you are for mercy. While you can't stop the messages of the world that can seem like crazy flying monkeys taunting you to do more, you can make your home a shelter from the storm. While our ultimate resting place promises to far outshine the Emerald City of Oz, our earthly lives don't have to be a sepia-toned existence. The work of mercy to shelter the homeless isn't just about the destitute on our streets; it also calls us to create the kind of haven that left Dorothy clicking her heels while repeating: "There's no place like home."

As someone who often sleeps with earplugs jammed in my ears because of my teenage son's proclivity to run kitchen appliances during late night study sessions, I admit that my home is not always restful. Too often I fail at making my home a true respite from the outside world. Yet picking paint colors and Pinterest boards, smell-good candles, and fluffy throw pillows is much easier than handling the dynamics of living with completely different people, in completely different life stages, with completely different dietary preferences. As you know, these differences in our homes can lead to challenging moments. Yet these challenges shouldn't mean we can't find rest in our homes. Even with our differences, home should be a place to rest, reconnect, and reflect on what matters most by offering shelter from the messages of the world that emphasize external achievements as the measurement of our value.

When I was a kid, the word "average" meant you were like everyone else. It meant you were okay. You were enough. You fell into the middle and didn't worry about being out-twirled at baton practice or made fun of when the metal bar fell on your head. At some point, though, everything changed. Being average now means that you are like the less-than sign used in math — pointing in the wrong direction, open to the mundanity of mediocrity. A losing symbol in a world that equates greatness with worthiness. Today's young people have so much pressure to perform, outshine, and overachieve. Many of them are only home long enough to eat, bathe, and sleep. They may have adequate physical shelter, but they are desperate for the respite of a place to decompress from the pressures of fitting in and measuring up.

While our worries may center on creating havens of peace for our families, others experience the devastation of physical homelessness. Far more pressing than a refuge from society's storms, the homeless lack even a safe place to sleep at night. The problem of homelessness is murky, often obscured by the fog of mental illness, drug addiction, affordable housing, choice, poverty, and unemployment. It's easy to feel overwhelmed by the needs of the homeless when most of us are struggling to meet the needs in our own homes. While we should always be alert and on the lookout for opportunities to help the homeless, we can begin practicing this work of mercy in our daily lives. Saint Teresa of Calcutta put it simply when she said, "We think sometimes that poverty is only being hungry, naked, and homeless. The poverty of being unwanted, unloved and uncared for is the greatest poverty. We must start in our own homes to remedy this kind of poverty."

HOME RUN

I understand football about as well as algebra. So, when I interviewed former NFL player Mark Brunell for a news article, I was grateful it wasn't about football. The Mark Brunell Charitable Foundation sponsored an overnight camp for local foster children, so they could enjoy the camaraderie and fun of a typical summer camp. I met some of the approximately one hundred campers, ranging in ages from six to fifteen, including a boy named Christian. He was seven and small for his age, wearing jeans and a gray hoodie that matched his eyes. I tried to coax a smile from his tiny mouth, but it was zipped like his jacket. I introduced him to my boys, telling him that my youngest was eight. Thinking, since they were close in age, they would be fast friends. Christian answered my questions with remarkable brevity. While asking about his brother, I accidentally referred to Christian's age as eight. With a flicker of excitement, he reminded me he was seven. "That's right! It's my boy that's eight!" I exclaimed. "I should try to remember that," I said with a smile. Finally, he smiled back. It was worth the wait.

If Christian was small for his age, then Harry, age fourteen was ginormous. He wore a green-and-yellow football jersey, a SpongeBob hat, and enormous red sneakers the same size as his age. Initially he didn't want to go to camp. "Now I love it," Harry said with a smile. Harry liked sports and participated in the Special Olympics. He had a genuine gentleness that belied his physical size. Harry said he had good sportsmanship, and I congratulated him since I am a terrible loser. When his friends walked past, he told them he would be in the newspaper. He wants to be a famous basketball player. I told him I would make sure he was in the newspaper and he would be famous just by being Harry. He responded with a ginormous smile.

Finally, Brunell spoke. He talked about baseball, the national passion, and the iconic George Herman "Babe" Ruth Jr. who made the country and the world fall in love with a simple stick, a ball, and the glorious sound of the crack when they collide. After explaining Babe Ruth's significance — winning seven pennants and four World Series — Brunell threw the classic curveball: Babe Ruth was a foster kid. He grew into greatness, and the message was clear: There was no reason this room full of kids couldn't either. "When I look at you, each one of your faces, I see greatness. I see the potential for you to go and change our world," Brunell said. I couldn't help but silently cheer him on. He told the children his favorite Bible verse. "For surely I know the plans I have for you," says the Lord. "Plans for your welfare and not for harm, to give you a future with hope" (Jer 29:11). He explained that the verse isn't just for people who read the Bible or football players, but for all of us. "Don't think for a second that because of where you are in your life, you can't be great. Don't think that you can't make a difference," Brunell said, gaining momentum like a baseball player running toward home plate. "Everyone has hopes and dreams. Believe that the future is bright, that God has a plan for you. Have hope." However you score it, whatever game you compare it to, Brunell's message is a win.

Encouraging those who come from broken or troubled homes can offer life-changing hope. While we may not all be able to formally foster children, we can be hospitable to neighborhood kids, our adult friends' children, and the friends and teammates of our own children. By participating in mentoring programs, coaching, and teaching, we are fostering the love and self-worth of home. Making children feel welcome, showing genuine interest in their lives, and offering them a safe place to be themselves, are all ways to share the best attributes of home — those that come from the heart.

> *"And Jesus said to him,*
> *'Foxes have holes, and*
> *birds of the air have*
> *nests; but the Son of*
> *Man has nowhere to lay*
> *his head.'"*
>
> *(Matthew 8:20)*

HOMESICK

I grew up in the eighties, when Cyndi Lauper's "Girls Just Want to Have Fun" was a favorite song. As a middle-aged woman, I just want a nap. I mean they're pretty fun, too, right? In retrospect, I don't know how fun life was for me growing up. My parents were divorced, and I was a latch-key kid living off Stouffer's frozen fettuccine dinners, ice cream bars, and Cool Whip. With all the confusion, angst, and acne that accompanies adolescence, belonging was more important to me than having fun. I felt like an astronaut floating around in a space suit trying to find my people — and more so, trying to find myself. Not all of us had the ideal homes we wanted as children or the homes we desire for our own children. Yet we have this innate longing for the mercy of home — a place where we are cherished, accepted, and find respite from the worries of the world.

Being homesick isn't just about missing home. Sometimes it's about what's missing in our homes. Each of us is unique, and our needs are too. What matters to one kid may be insignificant to another. Some children require more help with homework, social skills, or excess energy. For parents it can feel overwhelming to discern not only what a particular family member needs but how to accommodate it, especially considering the demands on our time and whatever perceived deficiencies we already feel compelled to make up for. Wherever we fall short, if we shelter our families under the umbrella of God's unconditional love, they will be covered by his abundance.

Building a family on a foundation of faith fills the gaps of our shortcomings — and as a mother, I realize I have plenty of shortcomings! Maybe I watched too many episodes of *The Brady Bunch* as a kid, but I had no idea motherhood would be so frazzling. Carol Brady was always calm and perfectly coiffed. But then she never had to be in two carpool lines on two different sides of town *at the same time* like I do. Sometimes I think I should have celebrity status as a sort of modern-day time traveler. And I'm not the only one. Today, the demands on parents and children have escalated like those groovy stairs in the Brady House. Raising kids in an era where technology has replaced Technicolor poses unique challenges. Our children need protection from the outside world where negative messages storm down, clouding judgment and dampening spirits. Nowhere is it more important to model Christ's unconditional love than in your home, where you can shelter loved ones with forgiveness, understanding, acceptance, and renewal. The notion of being a domestic goddess is as outdated as bell bottom pants. God doesn't care about our Instant Pots. He is concerned with the eternal. Until our hearts can be with him, we can make our homes havens from a weary world, not only for our families, but for anyone who comes under our roof.

HOMEWARD BOUND

I once volunteered to conduct surveys at a women's shelter as part of a census designed to learn about the needs of the homeless. What I learned shattered the stereotypes I had. Almost all of the women I interviewed were currently employed or seeking work — in retail, customer service, and even in our schools. Often these jobs only paid minimum wage. One woman told me she works as hard as a Hebrew slave, for almost nothing. Another woman told me she had spent the entire day applying for jobs. Clearly, they were not looking for a handout.

One of the questions the survey asked was: *What is the main reason you would say that you are homeless?* Sometimes the answer was domestic violence, but just as often it was mental illness — women struggling with depression or bipolar disorder. One woman lost her apartment in a fire. Another left a five-bedroom house in a different state to find out the person she moved here with was unreliable. Someone else told me she had a problem with me saying she was homeless, since she was living at the shelter. I apologized, realizing how hard it must be for her. One resident I spoke with went on a mini rant about racism. In the next breath, she said that if she doesn't like you because you are white, she will tell you. It underscored the absurdity of racism. I was sympathetic, and she softened as she shared her experiences.

More than anyone, it was a woman in her early thirties who embodied my experience learning about the homeless. She walked in and stood for an awkward moment before asking if this was where the surveys were being done. I had assumed she worked at the shelter because she looked lovely in a white linen shirt and perfectly pressed gray pleated skirt. How strange to see the stereotypical girl-next-door in a homeless shelter. I pictured her walking downtown, blending in seamlessly with the other working men and women. For many of these women, it was their first experience of homelessness, but there were others like her, who had grown up in foster care, spending their lives schlepping from one home to the next. She told me she was surprised when one former foster family reached out to her on Facebook. She called it both nice and weird. Although I only got a glimpse into these women's lives, it was enough to make me realize the importance of tearing down stereotypes of the homeless so I could be more compassionate and willing to serve.

SHELTER FROM THE STORM

While the last thing I need in life is more spinning, I took a spin class at the gym. Riding a stationary bike to nowhere while the instructor spits out a mix of commands and motivational platitudes is not my favorite thing to do. When I caught my breath long enough to utter a word, I began talking to the girl next to me. She was younger, prettier, and unlike me, could string together an entire sentence without gasping. *She was also homeless.* A victim of domestic abuse, she told me the CliffsNotes® version of her life, which included graduating from college with honors, joining the military, serving as a police officer, and returning to school for a nursing degree. Her voice quivered when she said she was living in a shelter, hiding from her abuser. As is typical for many in domestic abuse situations, she didn't have friends or contact with her family. Not knowing what to say, I listened, offered her my hand, and introduced myself. We walked out of the gym together like two ordinary girlfriends, headed to two very different homes.

"My people will abide in a peaceful habitation, / in secure dwellings, and in quiet resting places."

(Isaiah 32:18)

My interactions with the homeless always leave me humbled — not by how little they have but by how much we are alike. I am astounded to learn that many of them have jobs, or even, in the case of the girl I met at spin class, a gym membership. Society often uses stereotypes to justify ignoring the homeless. Saint Francis of Assisi is said to have warned, "If you have men who will exclude any of God's creatures from the shelter of compassion and pity, you will have men who deal likewise with their fellow men."

There are ways to uphold the dignity of the homeless even without providing them shelter. When we avert our eyes from someone who appears homeless, we lose sight of their humanity, and as a result, our own. Instead of quickening your pace, slow down, make eye contact, and smile. Be open to a chance to encounter God, to share his love, and imitate the profound compassion he offers. One of the most significant ways we can serve the homeless is by simply acknowledging them. Remember, even the King of Kings experienced homelessness. Jesus was born in a manger. He began life in exile, sheltered only by the love of a select few. Likewise, he died exposed and in public, and was buried in a grave that did not belong to him. Both the starkness of his birth and death serve as reminders that where we dwell isn't as important as who dwells within us.

HOME IS WHERE THE HEART IS

Sheltering at home became a unique challenge during the coronavirus pandemic. Being quarantined reminded me of the pet birds we kept when I was growing up. My friends hated spending the night at my house because the birds would squawk and squeal like angry alarm clocks way before our teenage bodies were ready to wake. And no wonder the birds were angry — they existed in a cage of monotony. I tried to have a good attitude about the necessary sacrifices of living during a pandemic. I considered mask-wearing a clever and inexpensive way to hide wrinkles, with the added benefit of no longer worrying about whether bits of salad were caught in my teeth. I pretended my stint at homeschooling was like a long (albeit dysfunctional) episode of *Little House on the Prairie*. I put away the Pinterest-worthy tchotchkes on the desk so my now work-from-home husband could actually use it. I did the FaceTime happy hours, the socially distanced visits in the sweltering back yard, and the scavenger hunt for mundanities such as toilet paper, disinfectant, and flour. Around noon each day, I pretended my nightgown was a sundress and carried on with the day's inactivity. I crammed peanut M&M's in my face and watched with envy as the hummingbird outside the window fluttered from flower to flower in a fury of freedom.

Even so, I recognized the unexpected gifts of the pandemic. The shuttered churches, businesses, and schools were a sober reminder of death's hunt and, more importantly, the often-unrecognized value of life. While the circumstances for quarantine were dire, it offered us time to consider living more deliberately. Surprisingly, with life's excess stripped away, we were left with *more*. We had more time with our families. We were running around town less and walking in our neighborhoods more. We weren't striving to meet others' expectations, but instead slowing enough to reconsider our own. While physically distancing from friends, we grew closer to them. We were commuting less and prayerfully contemplating more.

While life as we knew it shut down, hearts opened in ways that showed the generosity, creativity, and compassion that once seemed dormant among general society. There was a renewed, concerted effort to care for and protect others. Even with the despair and death brought by this virus, we have been reminded that we can choose the kind of life we want for ourselves and our family. We don't have to constantly react to the wave of secular society that pulls us under, often drowning our innate desire to love and serve God and our neighbor.

As of this writing, many of the restrictions imposed by governments to combat the coronavirus remain. This gives us an opportunity to focus on doing this work of mercy within our homes by resurrecting family dinners, rosaries, and service to those most affected by the quarantine. Regardless of your circumstances or the pandemic, by holding tight to the seeds of your Christian faith, you will never be like a caged bird. And it's under the shelter of our homes that we can best nourish and cultivate this faith.

Your home is a place to practice mercy in every season and every circumstance. Through conversation, the kind-

> *"In my Father's house there are many dwelling places. If it were not so, would I have told you that I go to prepare a place for you?"*
>
> *(John 14:2)*

ness of service, and the practice of compassion, you can draw closer to Christ through daily opportunities to love those sheltered in your home. Like Dorothy following the yellow brick road to the Emerald City of Oz, the works of mercy are a path to lead us to our true home — eternity with God. We don't have to wait for heaven to live in the haven of God's love. By practicing mercy, we can live like true heirs of Christ even when our homes feel crazier than Kansas during a twister. By making a home for Christ in our hearts, spending time in the haven of our churches, and building our families on a foundation of merciful love, we are certain to construct a life of genuine contentment.

MERCY WORKS: TRY IT

The American poet Robert Frost said, "Home is the place where, when you have to go there, they have to take you in." Who are you willing to take in for God? Whether it's the homeless on the street or the members of your own family, you can make your heart more hospitable to serving God through your neighbor.

- *In your home*: Prayer unites us within our families and in the congregation of the world's church family. Make family prayer a priority. When your spouse isn't the ideal roommate, don't complain. Offer up the small annoyances of dirty dishes and undone chores. Limit technology so everyone has respite from the constancy of email, social media, and the escapism of streaming video and games. Donate excess furnishings and household goods to organizations that serve the homeless. Invite stillness with books, quiet conversation, and games. Be present. Notice when someone seems down, aloof, angry, or lonely and shelter them in compassion.

- *In your community*: Honor the dignity of the homeless. Make eye contact. Say hello. Buy them a cup of coffee or a bite to eat. Volunteer at the animal shelter, nursing home, shelters, and foster care centers. Donate or volunteer at food pantries, soup kitchens, or homeless shelters. Consider your own gifts and use them to help resolve the issue of homelessness. Can you help with job placement, resumes, or coaching? Can you provide mental health services, companionship, or share the word of God? Collect socks, underwear, and toiletries to help with their basic needs. You might even prayerfully discern whether your family is in a position to consider taking in a foster child.

- *In your personal relationship with God*: Pray about what it means to have God abide in your heart. Think of your life as the temple that can minister to people through daily interactions. Create a space for daily prayer, Bible study, and solitude to build a closer relationship with Christ. Make your church your spiritual home. Know it is a sacred place of comfort, safety, and genuine rest.

REFLECTION QUESTIONS

In what ways can you and your spouse ensure a strong foundation of faith for your family?

In what ways — good and bad — has your own childhood influenced your family interactions? How can those experiences help you to be intentional about creating the ideal home for your family?

How can you challenge stereotypes of the homeless to inspire others to help serve them?

PRAYER

Dear Jesus, you came into this world homeless and you died exposed to the cruelty of mankind so that we would know the compassion of your love. Please unite us to your suffering and those who long for physical shelter. Help us to be vessels of your love, sharing your light with others so that they may know you abide in us and will desire to abide in you. May we live merciful lives so we can someday share your heavenly home and the eternity of your love.

5

Visit the Sick

"Let us understand that God is a physician,
and that suffering is a medicine for salvation,
not a punishment for damnation."

Saint Augustine

My dear friend Laura was diagnosed with stage IV lung cancer. It was beyond understanding how this exemplary woman, a young mother of two boys, could be gravely ill. Family and friends were in shock, heartsick over the treatment protocol she would endure and the grim prognosis. The community that loved her went to work immediately preparing meals, providing childcare, doing laundry, and cleaning her house. Mercy showed up big for Laura. Mercy was in the money raised for her medical expenses. Mercy was in the visits to the hospital, rides to chemo, and dedicated hospice care. Mercy was in the Mass celebrated in her bedroom surrounded by family during her last days. It was a beautiful example of the Body of Christ uniting to heal the body of someone so desperately loved. Yet after her passing, I wasn't thinking about mercy. It was grace that came to mind.

Laura accepted mercy with such grace. Before her illness, I understood the connotation of grace, but not its meaning. Grace was pretty and frilly and made an excellent name. I knew pat phrases like "by the grace of God" and "in good graces," but not what they meant. The more I explored mercy, the more I heard about grace. Mercy and grace are like opposite sides of the same coin, both given freely by God while paying exponential dividends. In a text I asked Laura to explain grace. She wrote, "God provides you with it every day. It's the patience you give your sweet kids. His grace and mercy are the only things that get me through the day." To know Laura was to know grace. Even when she was near death, she had an im-

> *"So we do not lose heart.*
>
> *Even though our outer*
>
> *nature is wasting away,*
>
> *our inner nature is being*
>
> *renewed day by day. For*
>
> *this slight momentary*
>
> *affliction is preparing*
>
> *us for an eternal weight*
>
> *of glory beyond all*
>
> *measure."*
>
> *(2 Corinthians 4:16–17)*

possible glow. She radiated grace, touching so many of us with her light. In another text she wrote, "God's glory is shining so big through all of this." So it was. It certainly shined in her. And like the lyrics of the 1779 hymn, *Amazing Grace*, all I could think was "how precious did that grace appear the hour I first believed."

By caring for others, we not only help heal the sick, we also receive special graces that bring us in union with God — in effect, healing our own weary souls. Visiting the sick gives us an opportunity to comfort others. By acting compassionately, we grow closer to God. The world prescribes self-care as medicine for weary hearts and restless souls. It suggests we pour a glass of wine and binge-watch Netflix. It tells us if God really existed there would be no sickness, suffering, or pain. It's a sticky lie coated in syrup that is so much easier to take than watching someone you love suffer with an illness. Yet God's healing surpasses the momentary bodily afflictions we endure. It's eternal — a medicine that doesn't merely offer temporary relief but a true cure for earthly sufferings. It's a chance to merge mercy and grace into the balm of salvation. My friend Laura understood this. During her illness, despite her weakness, amidst her undeserved suffering, she taught many this invaluable lesson. Amazing grace, indeed.

HEARTSICK

Sometimes I feel like a tiny bird with an injured leg from an encounter with the claws of a crazed cat. I know how lucky I am to be here and how much worse things could be; yet still my wounds keep me tethered to the ground. Mental anguish, lack of faith, depression, and despair can make us physically and spiritually sick. It isn't always obvious to others or even ourselves when we need help. We still show up for work or in the carpool line. We paint a smile on our face with lipstick while our insides may feel numb, inadequate, and empty.

When I felt a persistent indifference about life, I ignored it. A few people noticed I lost weight, one friend sent me to her hormone doctor, and another one tried to rationalize my random crying episodes by saying everyone feels like that sometimes. The problem was "sometimes" had become every day. Finally, I saw my doctor who tried to diagnose me with depression. I was adamant that the problem was with my hormones or my thyroid or my cat's effects on my REM sleep cycle, because technically I had nothing to be unhappy about. Tears streamed down my face as I denied my sadness and recited a litany of my blessings. Now, it's almost comical to think about. *My life is good. I've already cried easily. Just give me some extra hormones and I will be fine.* Thankfully, she persisted and I got help.

Suffering can feel like a metastasizing cancer spreading misery faster than any work of mercy can offer relief. We question God. We seek answers and meaning in an infinite internet search. We can become so lost in the darkness that we are blind to the light manifesting through it. By valuing and prioritizing the mental health of those in society, we can be that light for others. Helping the heartsick acknowledge their grief, listening without judgment, and encouraging professional help can make a profound difference. Sharing your own story of pain can make someone feel less alone, while also facilitating your own healing.

Life can feel as relentless as a marathon, as we hop along like that tiny bird with the injured leg. One of my favorite quotes is from Saint John Paul II, who said: "We are an Easter people and Alleluia is our song." It conveys such unparalleled joy — a skyward ascent of heavenly praise. It hardly makes me think of hopping. Yet all of life's heartache from death, sin, rejection, and remorse can feel too austere for an alleluia song. It may not always feel like it, but your time on earth is nothing but a rising. Even when it's hard or feels impossible — when there is not enough money, not enough time, not enough of your poor, tired soul to go around — be strong and rise. Your suffering does not define you. Challenge, adversity, and illness cannot stop your ascent. It's not just Christ's resurrection you have to celebrate, it's the possibility of your own. Easter isn't just a day that marks the end of Lent. It's an everyday. The shedding of your burdens, the surrendering of suffering at the foot of Jesus' cross, service to others, and the unification of

"A joyful heart is good medicine, / but a crushed spirit dries up the bones."

(Proverbs 17:22, ESV)

your soul to his, is what makes your rising possible. It's what helps us to remember that even in our brokenness, we are an Easter people, and we still have wings to fly. Alleluia.

THE BEST MEDICINE
If you recall, age eleven can be tough. There is funky stuff going on with your body, you're a tad emotional, and you vacillate between knowing exactly who you are and not having a clue. (It's eerily similar to middle-age.) I met my best friend, Kelley, when I was eleven years old. We signed all of our novel-length notes BFF (Best Friends Forever) and even shared pieces of a jagged half-heart necklace with the best friend sentiment engraved. While the necklace was a bit "You complete me," à la Tom Cruise to Renée Zellweger in the movie *Jerry Maguire*, it also meant I was part of something bigger than myself, and who doesn't want that?

Years later Kelley reached out to me to help her find a Bible verse for a project for her friend whose eleven-year-old daughter was diagnosed with a reoccurrence of cancer. They were making a *Ring of Encouragement* that included Scripture verses pertaining to hope and healing. In it are pictures of friends next to the

Bible verse they chose as a prayer offering for the young girl. It made me smile to think of her looking at the pictures of people all over the country, who love her, are praying for her, and believe in her healing. That seems like the best kind of medicine. Like that half-heart necklace, I wanted to be a part of it. I didn't think it mattered that the young girl didn't know me, or that I was someone who came to know her brave fight from a friend I first met at the same age she is now. Maybe it mattered more that she didn't know me, that someone she's never met was praying for her. I asked everyone I knew to share a Bible verse, inspiring quote, or encouraging message, so she would know there were many people praying for her healing. In addition, I asked people to consider donating money to help pay for her medical expenses. People were generous in word and deed — the best pieces of all of us sending a healing message that was all heart.

Serving the sick is one of the hardest acts of love. It's hard to believe that something as beautiful as grace has anything to do with cleaning bodily fluids off the bathroom floor. When we have been awake all night with a sick child, haven't bathed in a few days, and aren't sure if that's a rash developing around our eyes or just irritation from the sleepless nights crusting in the crevice of a new wrinkle, we hardly feel graceful. Instead, as we seek to show mercy, we worry about the right medicines, doses, ointments, and medical advice. We worry that our loved one won't improve. We worry that we won't know when to take them to the emergency room, specialist, or just out for fresh air.

Comforting the sick is often unplanned. We feel unprepared. It can be exhausting and scary, and it rearranges everything in our carefully scheduled day planners. My oldest son was fourteen months old when he had his first seizure. He fell back in my arms, convulsing. I called 911 and ran into the front yard holding my limp child, looking skyward, and begging God for his healing. Waiting for the paramedics was agony. The mercy they showed when they arrived — offering me comfort and him care — was the gift of grace. It wasn't frilly or fancy. It looked like an unshowered, terrified mother in pajamas, being shuttled off in an ambulance sick with worry, but trusting that God had heard her plea. Turning to God with prayers for healing for the sick, and with our own worries as caretakers, remedies more than just physical ailments. It offers us the health of peace regardless of our circumstances.

Frequently the service we are called to do is organic, and, like the produce in the grocery store, organic always costs more. It has always felt easier to serve when I plan for it, choose the capacity, and have had a shower. When someone else's misfortune interrupts my plans or to-do list, it can be frustrating. One day my mom was sick and asked me to take her to the doctor. I tried to be peppy about it despite my manic Monday mentality. I wondered why serving God was sometimes so hard. Why couldn't I do this small thing with joy when my mom has done countless things for me? After all, I know that it's a work of mercy to care for the sick. But maybe the answer to that question doesn't matter. What is significant is that I did it anyway. Of course, I wish I had done it more selflessly and joyfully knowing that I was doing something pleasing to God and helpful to my mother. For my own sake, as much as anyone else's, I wish I welcomed every opportuni-

> *"Let us therefore approach the throne of grace with boldness, so that we may receive mercy and find grace to help in time of need."*
>
> *(Hebrews 4:16)*

ty to serve knowing that the mercy I extend has been extended to me 1,000-fold by our heavenly Father.

PRESCRIPTION TO SERVE

Can you imagine an ambulance taking your spouse to the hospital, him joking with the paramedics one second, and his eyes rolling back the next? Your pulse races; his stops. The paddles shock life back into his body. It's an unsettling scenario. It was also my mom's life for almost five years after her husband was diagnosed with cancer. There were surgeries, chemo, radiation, staph infections, pneumonias, and MRSA, among other things.

My mom married Bob when I was pregnant with my first son. At twenty-nine years old, I wasn't interested in having a stepdad. It was too weird at my age to think of having another parent. Still, I considered him a blessing. He was there when I gave birth, when my dog died, and when my kids were sick. He and my mom would let me tag along with them when my kids were small, and I was lonely. He would send encouraging notes about my writing and I would hang them on my bulletin board. He always signed them, "Daddy Bob." Regardless of my initial hesitation, that's what I and the rest of my family ended up calling him, thanks to my son who couldn't say Granddaddy Bob.

I tried to care for him mostly by helping my mom. I cooked, cleaned, picked up prescriptions and groceries, cared for pets, sat with her in the ER, the hospital, and at doctors' appointments. I answered middle-of-the-night phone calls and lifted him when he needed help up the steps or off the floor. Mostly, he stayed in his bedroom and rarely wanted visitors. At first this hurt my feelings, but then it became a relief. It was easier to serve on the other side of the door. One day I visited him in the hospital. He was physically different, worn, and wasted. It was awkward seeing him so weak and I had to catch my breath. He started crying when he saw me. He thanked me for coming and said he was happy to see me. He got so excited when I talked to him about the boys. I tried to stay composed. I looked away and thought momentarily about how people talk about telling loved ones what they mean to them while they still have the chance. I had done it before and couldn't manage to do it again that day. Before I left, I kissed him goodbye and told him I love him.

When I got home, I went to a large statue of the Blessed Virgin Mary, Our Lady of Fatima, in my dining room. It is known as the traveling statue of Our Lady. Pope John Paul II wanted a statue of Our Lady of Fatima to be in every parish because of his devotion to Mary and the Rosary. The statue travels to different homes so that families can pray the Rosary. Standing in front of her, I thought about our call to comfort the sick. I thought of my mother's devotion and selflessness. I thought of Mary's own suffering, watching her son die on the cross. She never walked away, as hard as it must have been to watch the torment of her child. She stayed. Love compels you to serve despite the challenges involved. It gives you the strength to step up, to keep going, to endure for as long as necessary. That's what Mary did for Jesus and what my mom did for her husband. In honor of them both, I took the rosary from our Blessed Mother's hands into my own and began to pray for Daddy Bob's comfort, "now until the hour of his death."

A SPOONFUL OF LAUGHTER
HELPS THE MEDICINE GO DOWN

There are many ways we can comfort the sick. We can bring them a meal, pick up prescriptions, take them to the doctor, make care packages, visit, pray, or watch their children. However, the most important way to serve is by listening and respecting the sick person's wishes. They may want solitude, prefer their regular routine, or find meal delivery intrusive. By modifying our acts of love to accommodate the sick, we can offer true comfort. Being other-centric means putting aside our own notion of service and considering the individual we aim to help. Comforting the sick is a prescription that offers healing to both the giver and receiver. Taking care of a sick loved one gives us an opportunity to stop the routine of daily life and show the same compassion that we so often have been shown. Sometimes Jesus healed with his touch. Other times, with his words. Always, he healed with love. So can we.

My friend Laura lived with persistent positivity despite her illness. She knew she needed a miracle, and while that would feel daunting to most people, she absolutely believed if it were God's will, she would be that miracle. I was lucky enough to say goodbye during her final days. I don't think she understood my sadness because, either way, she knew she was going to be a miracle. Either way, she was going to be redeemed by God. The miracle wasn't manifest in the way those who loved her wanted. We wanted her to live with us, raise her babies, and love her husband. We wanted her to keep us laughing and lighthearted. Still, the way she united people in God's love, delighted in his hope, and refused to be defeated by despair was its own miracle.

> *"Heal the sick, raise the*
> *dead, cleanse lepers,*
> *cast out demons. You*
> *received without paying;*
> *give without pay."*
> *(Matthew 10:8, ESV)*

It wasn't just the grace with which Laura handled her sickness that was inspiring, it was the ease in which she lived life. She lived with the peace of a joyful heart. She put her trust in God, and even in sickness it did not disappoint. Her faith did not fail.

It came to fruition when she went to her heavenly home to rest in God's loving arms. In sickness or in health we all have a choice of how we handle suffering. We can choose to surrender to God's will and live with the joy of divine providence, or we can choose to live in fear and bitterness over what ails us and those we love. Laura chose joy.

MERCY WORKS: TRY IT
"Heal me, O Lᴏʀᴅ, and I shall be healed; / save me, and I shall be saved, / for you are my praise" (Jer 17:14, ESV). Let us show Jesus our praise by offering comfort to the sick, following his example.

- *In your home*: Teach your children how to care for sick family members. Have them make a home-made card, take over the chores of those who don't feel well, and ask sick family members how they can best comfort them. When taking care of sick children, spouses, or parents, remember that the mercy you show will manifest grace in your life. Use opportunities of compassion to draw closer to Christ's suffering and redemption. Pay attention to signs of depression or other mental illness in your spouse and children. Let them know that their mental health is as important as their physical health. Be vigilant to protect your family's spiritual health as well by keeping Christ in the center of your home. Cultivate holy joy in your home so your children will learn to rely on God, find gifts in their trials, and learn resilience from their sufferings.

- *In your community*: Raise money or collect books for the sick. Attend fundraisers that support the sick or dying. Visit the hospitalized, those in assisted living, and friends or neighbors who are ill. Set up a meal delivery sign-up for a sick friend. Pick up the slack for a sick coworker. If possible, accompany the sick to the doctor, take notes for them, and help with the logistics of their situation. Pray for the sick and rally others to do the same. If you are an extraordinary minister of Holy Communion, bring the Eucharist to the sick. If there is an emergency situation or the sickness is dire, call for a priest to administer the anointing of the sick. Donate blood. Use the opportunity to comfort the sick to share compassion as part of Jesus' discipleship. Where in-person visits are not possible, consider writing a card or giving a sick friend a call.

- *In your personal relationship with God*: Turn to God for hope and comfort when you or a loved one are sick. Do not fall into despair, but instead rise in your suffering to the glory that awaits. Offer up the hardship of caring for the sick. Ask for God's graces as you share his compassion with others. Surrender your fear and trust his will. Rejoice in the redemptive power of Christ. "And he said to her, 'Daughter, your faith has made you well; go in peace, and be healed of your disease'" (Mk 5:34, ESV).

REFLECTION QUESTIONS
What would you find most helpful if you or a loved one were seriously ill? Using those comforts, how can you help the sick?

Is there something in your life or the lives of those you love that is making you sick at heart? How can the word of God heal that anxiety or pain?

Has there been a time in your life where someone else came to your aid? Do you accept mercy with grace or is it hard for you to accept help? Pray with this question and ask God to help you receive mercy just as you seek to give it.

PRAYER

Dear Jesus, help me to imitate your example of compassion for the sick. Let me be a beacon of comfort to those who are ailing and a source of mercy to everyone I encounter. Give me the strength to serve others with joy so that I may receive the favor of your grace. Keep watch over me and those I love, and spare us from the hopelessness of despair. Help me to rejoice in the mercy of compassion and minister to others with joy in my heart.

6

Visit Prisoners

*"To have a right to do a thing is not at all
the same as to be right in doing it."*

G. K. Chesterton

To commemorate my fortieth birthday, I wanted to celebrate with a tiara, champagne, gondola ride, and miniature monkeys dressed in tuxedos fanning me. Instead, I went to prison. (There's always such discrepancy between my plans and God's.) Thankfully, I went as a guest and not because of an altercation between the fanning monkeys and me. I walked through the razor-sharp wires of Florida State Prison, down the long, silent hallway of death row, and into a prison prayer service without the protection of a prison guard. What I remember most about visiting death row was the broken light peeking in from the old jalousie windows across from the cells. Other than these shreds of natural light, it was dim, and many inmates remained in bed despite it being midday. While the light was bent from the horizontal slant of the window's glass, it refused to be kept out — as if it were trying to nudge awake those who had fallen asleep in despair. Seeing that light find its way into the darkness of prison reminded me of God's unconditional love and inexhaustible mercy.

The way I look at it, we're all in some kind of prison. There are the homebound sick, the elderly in nursing homes, the addicted, the lonely, and the abused. But mostly we're in prisons of our own making. Maybe it's a prison of self-judgment. Maybe you are in servitude to your job or your children. Maybe a health problem, anxiety, or depression holds you hostage. Maybe money, status, and prestige are your wardens. Perhaps you feel shackled to mistakes from your past. Over the course of my own personal year of mercy, I came to realize that my life without knowing God's mercy had been its own kind of prison. Visiting those in prison isn't only an invitation to minister to the imprisoned; it's also an opportunity to revisit old hurts and limiting thought patterns while contemplating the true redemption found in God's mercy.

> *"Remember those who are in prison, as though in prison with them, and those who are mistreated, since you also are in the body."*
>
> *(Hebrews 13:3, ESV)*

Mercy is the get-out-of-jail-free card we long for but don't deserve. We don't receive mercy by chance or a lucky roll of the dice. There aren't parameters or hierarchies to it. It pours out from our merciful Father. It's God's universal gift, bought at the heavy price of Jesus' suffering and death. The freedom God offers doesn't discriminate. Yet often, when it comes to sharing mercy, we do. Like the stereotypical garb worn by inmates, often our opinion of prisoners is black and white. Too often, we create a hierarchy for mercy, even if subconsciously, and for most of us, prisoners are at the bottom, the least deserving of our compassion since they intentionally hurt others. Far stronger than any bars that constrain are beliefs that the incarcerated deserve no thought, companionship, and certainly, no mercy. We often don't see the parallels between their situation and our own. While visiting those in prison can be a profound spiritual experience, you can start to practice this work of mercy by visiting what imprisons you and the people you love.

HOLD-UP

One evening when my son was fourteen months old, my husband and I left him playing with his grandparents while we went on a walk. Noticing a truck hovering behind us, I got up on the curb to give it room to pass. Without warning, the driver accelerated, roaring the engine and spinning his wheels toward us. With a slam of the brakes, his tires rested on the curb and the oversized truck sat eerily still. A young man wearing a skullcap jumped out of the truck's passenger side. Without hesitating, he stretched his arm, pointing his pistol sideways, and demanded that we get into his truck. Pulling me away from the gunman, my husband pushed me toward the neighbor's house. My steps felt awkward and strangely slow. As we both ran, my husband screamed, "No! No! PLEASE GOD, DON'T LET HIM KILL US! SOMEONE HELP US! PLEASE GOD!" The shrill sound of his voice shook me. His plea was to God. It was a prayer. It was filled with terror, desperation, and for sure, it was a cry for mercy. At any second, my family could be destroyed. Still using his body to direct me, my husband rushed us toward the neighbor's house where he pushed me over the porch railing. The gunman seemed as unsure as I did and stepped slowly toward us. Finally, my survival instincts kicked in, and I banged on the neighbor's window, screaming for help. I never saw the man get back into his truck, but I watched it drive away. It stopped three houses down the street. Our desperate pleas for help remained unanswered. It was agonizing. My husband and I felt like lost souls in purgatory ... waiting. Finally, the truck drove off.

"They promise them freedom, but they themselves are slaves of corruption; for people are slaves to whatever masters them."

(2 Peter 2:19)

While I was grateful to be alive, I wasn't the same after that. Always on guard, my heart racing and my mind frantic with what-ifs, I couldn't understand what had happened, or why I didn't react differently. I started doubting myself, and worse, my ability to protect my child. I hated that I was not like one of Charlie's Angels or Wonder Woman or that Kung Fu guy. The gunman was free, and I was imprisoned by fear, shame, and doubt from the experience. It was a long time before I finally understood that what happened didn't make me weak, helpless, or incapable. So often, we can be our worst enemies, creating unnecessary suffering instead of practicing the same mercy God shows

us. Like prison inmates, we too are often enslaved by our own doing. Only we don't always see what confines us. We build invisible
cells, block by block, out of fear, doubt, anger, sin, bitterness, and
jealousy. Only by letting these things go will we be free.

UNDER LOCK AND KEY

Men live in six- by nine-foot cells. They shower every other
day and only go outside a few times a week. When they do, they
remain completely fenced in an area akin to a dog run. Adult
men living on 1,500 calories of food per day, which is justified by their sedentary existence. Inmates can't even turn on
and off the lights in their cell or flush their own toilets. That's
left to the discretion of prison guards who control the inside
of their cells. Prisoners live without air-conditioning or heat. I
can't compare it to anything because I've never seen anything
like it until my visit to Florida State Prison. The deacon who
accompanied me told me stories of redemption, forgiveness,
and God's love that he witnessed while ministering to inmates.
He also shared horrors of brutal prison murders, rapes, and the
spread of HIV.

Entering a concrete world of metal bars, shackles, and bolts
made me reconsider my views toward the imprisoned. Like
many of us, I have experienced outrage from acts of violent
crime, causing me to confuse justice with retribution. It's far too
easy to see offenders only by their crime and turn a blind eye
to mercy. Moreover, I forget that God loves them as much as he
loves me, making me feel like the jealous brother in the parable
of the prodigal son. *Really, God? You love the axe murderer as
much as you love me? Don't you love me just a tiny bit more?* Visiting prisoners helped me get past my prejudices, discomfort, and
fear to that place of compassion which God, in his constancy, has
always shown.

I walked down the quiet hall on death row and tried not to

turn my head as my eyes strained sideways to catch glimpses of inmates as they appeared lifeless in their beds. When the deacon introduced me to the prisoners, he referred to them as his friends. One of them had been in prison thirty-two years. I wondered if he was a completely different person now that a generation had passed. The inmate spoke about letters he wrote to pen pals, how his oldest son had disowned him, and about God. Mostly, I liked him. He was socially appropriate, engaging, and seemed sincere. Later, I learned he drowned a ten-year-old girl.

So began my vacillating between feelings of compassion for their lack of freedom and dignity, to conflicting and valid justifications for their punishment. The injustice of murder, the depravity of torture, the senseless disregard for life, the endless grieving of victims' families — these were not things I could forget. As someone who values life, dignity, and decency, who spoke with these men, shared the Eucharist with them, prayed with them, shook their hands, listened to them, and laughed with them, I can't celebrate the fact that they live in a state-controlled hell, either. As badly as I want to have hope for those incarcerated, as much as I want to believe they would choose the forgiveness God offers — which even the state cannot take away — I am not naïve enough to think they all will. Yet the same can be said of those of us outside of prison.

The person I saw that day who most embodied God's unconditional love was an elderly lady waiting in the prison foyer. She had carefully applied bright pink lipstick and a rosy shade of blush to her cheeks, as if she were somehow applying the dew of happiness to her face instead of merely drugstore makeup. She wore dainty jeweled barrettes, which held back parts of her soft gray hair. Although I looked as asexual as an amoeba that day, I recognized the effort she put into her appearance. The deacon knew her and asked about her incarcerated son, kindly remarking that he was a good boy. As I watched her face twist in uncertainty and gratitude, all those shades of pink contorting until tears filled her eyes, my heart sank. She nodded despite the circumstances. Of course, her son was good because she knew him with a mother's love. How crushing it must be to know how the world sees him, to know the child she gave life to unmercifully took it from someone else. Later, in the visiting area, I watched her with her son. He seemed

"So if the son makes you free, you will be free indeed." (John 8:36)

like a shell of a person. Still, she drove 300 miles each way, every week, to visit him. Whatever he did, she still loved him.

After my visit, I looked up news articles about some of the death-row inmates. In one of them, I read about a mother who learned her daughter's killer was sentenced to death. She said her daughter would be dancing in heaven at the verdict. While I would never begrudge anyone the joy of a dance, when I think of these two mothers and the loss they both endure, I feel nothing but sorrow. I remind myself that as impenetrable as prison may be, nothing can restrain the hope of God's love. I remember the old lady and her pink cheeks. I picture her in a matching pink dress, cocooned in layers of tulle, dancing in heaven with her son, not as the world knew him, but as she did … a child of God redeemed by salvation. May their dance last for eternity.

RULE FOLLOWER
When my children were little, I took a painting class at the local high school with my mom. She was interested in painting and I was interested in an occasion to wear a clean shirt. I always thought of art as an easy breezy endeavor that you couldn't mess

up. I approached it with the carefree abandon of a finger-painting toddler. I listened to the teacher's instruction, disregarded it, and did what I wanted. I loved the bright colors and had such hope for what they would become. Swirling them together, adding more paint, different colors, and bigger swirls, I created what my teacher called mud — and that was just my pallet board. Frustrated, I whined to my teacher (and I am sure he wanted to drink a bottle of wine after we left). I told him that art shouldn't have rules. I've never forgotten his response. He said, "To create something beautiful, you have to know the rules, so you know when it's okay to break them."

Like many of us, I want to do what's easiest. I don't always want to follow rules. There are plenty of people in this world who will say that this is okay, even healthy. The world tells us that if we do what makes us happy, focus on instant gratification, and indulge in the decadence of our desires, we will have fulfillment. In Pope Francis's August 2014 address to the dioceses of Germany, he explained the danger of this distorted image of freedom:

> If it is not used well, freedom can lead us away from
> God, can make us lose the dignity with which he has
> clothed us. This requires the guidelines and the rules,
> both in society and in the Church, to help us do God's
> will, thus living according to our dignity as human be-
> ings and children of God. When it is not shaped by the
> Gospel, freedom can turn into slavery: the slavery of sin.

God created you to live in the fullness of freedom. When we chase worldly wants, strive for the standards set by mankind, and hold on to pain, resentment, and unhealthy habits, we surrender that freedom for a life spent chasing, seeking, striving, and stuck. The world often uses the concept of freedom to weaponize, destroy, control, and manipulate. As a result, the true meaning of freedom is lost. Our "me"-centric society believes freedom means having no standards of right or wrong; as a result, we unknowingly bind ourselves to the misery of sin. The Church's teachings aren't intended to constrain you but to protect you from hurting yourself and others. There are consequences to our actions, and for better or worse, they often spread beyond what we see. To paint a beautiful picture with our lives, we must keep our colors pure, vivid, and free from muddied living.

Many of us suffer from a limited existence. We may not be living behind prison bars, but we are held hostage by addiction, ambition, greed, materialism, anger, sadness, and sinfulness. To the person imprisoned by loneliness, sickness, or grief, small acts of kind-

"For you were called to freedom, brothers. Only do not use your freedom as an opportunity for the flesh, but through love serve one another. For the whole law is fulfilled in one word: 'You shall love your neighbor as yourself.'"

(Galatians 5:13–14, ESV)

ness are significant. Visiting those in less visible prisons may look like a conversation with a friend in an unhealthy relationship; offering support to someone who is struggling with sobriety; or helping your child understand the sometimes complicated dynamics of fitting in. Link by link, we forge chains that separate us from God when we look to the world to compensate for our desires, emptiness, and unworthiness. If we are willing to look to one another instead, we have the chance to embrace the divinity of God, grow closer to him, and discover that imitating his mercy offers the unparalleled freedom of genuine love. By visiting a nursing home, joining a prison ministry, or spending time with someone going through a difficult time, you not only visit the imprisoned, you also get a glimpse of the freedom that God offers through his uncontainable mercy.

MERCY WORKS: TRY IT

In his masterpiece *Mere Christianity*, C. S. Lewis wrote, "If a thing is free to be good it is also free to be bad. And free will is what has made evil possible. Why, then, did God give them free will? Because free will, though it makes evil possible, is also the only thing that makes possible any love or goodness or joy worth having." Let's use our free will to visit those who are physically and spiritually imprisoned.

- *In your home*: Make your home a place where freedom is used to love, nurture, respect, and rejoice by cultivating a place of acceptance. Validate your spouse and children, especially in areas where they are trying or feel particularly weak. Encourage family members to recognize the prisons in which they may be trapped, from anxiety about grades to sinful behaviors. Help them escape by turning to the Church's teachings on our inherent value and the peace of reconciliation. Have conversations about society's laws and God. Discuss where they overlap in protecting us, and where they diverge. Explain that what's legal isn't always right. God's law is sovereign. Use art to show your kids the parameters of freedom by creating something beautiful within the bounds of judicious rules. Practice forgiveness in all circumstances.

- *In your community*: Consider getting involved with a prison ministry. Some ministries actually visit those in prison, while others allow you to correspond with prisoners. Still others help those recently released from prison with the mercy of a fresh start. Advocate for decent prison conditions and write to lawmakers about the inhumanity of the death penalty. Visit the homebound, those in nursing homes, and the lonely. Be a mentor to troubled youth. Volunteer at legal aid or as a court-appointed guardian *ad litem*. Be a good citizen. Follow the law.

- *In your personal relationship with God*: Forgive yourself for your shortcomings, failures, and flaws. Know that God isn't focused on what you lack, but on how much you love. Love in abundance. Forgive others the way you have been forgiven. Set yourself free from perfectionism, materialism, and what others think of you. Concern yourself only with loving and serving God. Consider what separates you from him. Make the connection between service and the fulfillment of your soul. Remind yourself of the joy that awaits when you use your freedom to imitate the example set by Jesus.

REFLECTION QUESTIONS
Keeping in mind the merciful love of God, how can you address what imprisons you?

Using the concept of free will, how can you teach your children the merits of using freedom to live as Christians?

In what ways can you show compassion for the imprisoned? Are you able to visit them? In what other ways might God be calling you to notice and serve those who are imprisoned, whether behind bars or in other, more hidden ways?

PRAYER
Dear merciful Father, set me free from everything that separates me from you, most especially my sins. Help me to see with the eyes of the imprisoned the great gift of freedom that your mercy bestows. Help me to use it to serve you, to set others free, and to spread the seeds of your mercy, for I know that with the light of your love, there is no place it cannot grow.

7
Bury the Dead

"When he shall die, take him and cut him out in
little stars, and he will make the face of heaven
so fine that all the world will be in love with
night and pay no worship to the garish sun."

William Shakespeare

I lost my dear friend, Teresa, unexpectedly. It was a Tuesday in Lent, and I'd planned to go to the grocery store. Instead, I headed to the emergency room, where hope dissolved into death. She had the flu. More importantly, she had two young daughters and a devoted husband. I tried to comfort their shattered hearts, to absorb the magnitude and finality of Teresa's death, and to find words that conveyed the illogical reality of her loss as I shared the news with friends. Suddenly, the ashes spread thick on my forehead in the shape of a cross almost two weeks before on Ash Wednesday had new meaning. They no longer represented the inevitability of death, but the actuality of it. It was no longer a someday, but a very unexpected today.

Losing Teresa was a darkness that went beyond black. Despite this, I know the promise of eternal life that awaits the end of the Lenten season was fulfilled. She encountered Easter. The gift of Easter, beyond the white lilies and choruses of jubilant alleluias, outside the pastel dresses and the wide-brimmed hats, sweeter than the chocolate in wicker baskets or the smiles of delight they invoke, is the resurrection of the Son of God, who suffered, died, and was buried so that we could live perpetually. His rising wipes clean the black ash of sufferings, grief, and sorrow, so that we no longer know death but are assured life. The work of mercy to bury the dead transforms the emptiness of ash into exaltation, eternity, and love everlasting.

Despite death's inevitability, it never makes its way into our day planners. Its physiology is simple. Yet for the grieving, simplicity is a satire. Few things feel more complicated than burying the dead. There is so much to plan, yet death is rarely planned. There are decisions to be made in a situation that no one chose. There are people to tell when the truth is unspeakable. There is a celebration of life to attend amidst mourning. It's a blur for the bereaved, who seek to honor a life's entirety while trying not to totally fall apart. Long after the funeral arrangements have been finalized, the bereaved often endure an ongoing struggle to bury the dead emotionally. The world keeps moving even though it feels like everything has stopped. Grief is a slow-motion spin teetering between numb disbelief and absurd pain.

Burying the dead extends beyond funeral services and comforting the bereaved to burying the dead of your past so that you may rise to the life for which you have been called. You can't be who God intended — who the world desperately needs — while living in the muck of bad memories, poor choices, and self-criticism. There are countless ways to die that have nothing to do with a stopped heart. Burying the dead is as much about uncovering what has entombed you as it is putting to rest the pain of your past. The French military leader Napoleon Bonaparte said, "Death is nothing, but to live defeated is to die every day." The army of God was created for victory, and our rising comes from within our faith. Teresa has risen too, and because she lived seeking

> *"For everything there is a season, and time for every matter under heaven."*
>
> *(Ecclesiastes 3:1)*

and exuding light, I have risen higher for knowing her. I rejoice for the one who gave his only Son, the one who blessed me with a friend so dear that I learned that Easter isn't only a Sunday marking the end of Lent, but a rebirth we encounter every day in the people we love.

GOOD GRIEF

I had been to four funerals in almost as many months. I tried to find light from each of the lives I mourned, to formulate a takeaway, some kind of life lesson that would make sense of all the sorrow. I did okay at first, feeling a heightened gratitude for my life and the people in it. The gift of death is that it edges life, delineating what matters most. Because of sorrow, we see more clearly, act more deliberately, and love more purposefully. All the unimportant things that usually consume us are momentarily deemed inconsequential. The stark contrast between life and death offers us a clearer perspective and realigns our priorities. With all this newfound enlightenment, I figured I would be ablaze with the word of God. Instead, I felt numb. I craved normalcy, but I was unsure what that looked like anymore. Families that are dear to me lost mothers and fathers, and I lost cherished friends. Carrying this new reality folded up reverently and tucked away in the gap created by the loss in my heart, I attempted to move on. Occasionally, I paused to unfold my grief, look at it in disbelief, and wept for a love that was once tangible.

Without love, there would be no mourning. As the poet Emily Dickinson wrote, "Unable are the loved to die for love is immortality." Love isn't only the romance and roses the world portrays. It can also be difficult decisions, sleepless nights, and gut-wrenching sorrow as you try to comprehend the incomprehensible finality of death. With bittersweet longing, we remember our beloved, keeping the comfort of Jesus' resurrection close. He offers the hope of eternal life, when grief will finally be put to rest.

SKELETONS IN THE CLOSET

I sometimes wonder who I would be if certain hurts had not happened. I know that sounds like a tortuous exercise of would've, could've, should've best reserved for a rainy-day pity party. Yet it's important to acknowledge that some experiences change us. It's not transformation we should fear. After all, God changed death into life. Instead, it's living with the skeletons of our grief. By burying betrayal, regret, grief, and disillusionment, we have a chance to live in the hope of now. When we cling to our wounds, we experience an unnatural death that keeps us from living fully.

Loss is a part of our human experience. It's when we don't grieve and properly bury our hurts and disappointments that we become entombed in suffering. When you feel stuck, you may stay in unhealthy relationships, discount your worth and the value of others, and experience a general mistrust and sense of cynicism. Holding on to hurt, resentments, and lost opportunities prolongs your suffering and limits your relationships, your sense of peace, and your willingness to help others. Despite your losses, by choosing healing over hate you can inspire others to do the same. You can choose redemption over resentment, altruism over anger, and trust over fear. By loving through loss, you choose life. And always, you should choose life.

During times of despair or when our spiritual life feels more dead than dormant, it can feel as if God has abandoned us. Jesus is hibernating in our hearts and we ache for him to warm the world's chill. Somber seasons of life can remind us of the fear and abandonment Jesus felt in the Garden of Gethsemane. During such times, it's important to trust as Jesus did, and to pray with him, *Thy will be done.* To embrace the life God meant for us, we must acknowledge our pain and let go of what we think our lives should look like. You can help your neighbors do this too by showing concern for their suffering, suggesting devotions, and offering to pray with and for them. Jesus suffered beyond the comprehensible and yet it wasn't what defined him. From conception through infinity that was always love — not loss.

WHY, GOD?

Ten Burmese refugees in a van were on their way home from work at a chicken-processing plant when a wrong-way driver hit them. The father of the van's driver and the man sitting behind him died. Five others were in critical condition. It was a tragedy that left me questioning, *Why, God?* Why did these people, working to have a better life, have to suffer such anguish? Deciding that what to do now mattered more than why, I reached out to someone who works with the Burmese community and offered to help by cooking, watching children, providing transportation, visiting the hospital, or assisting with funeral services. I was asked to help with the funeral and put in touch with Sonny, another refugee who would introduce me to the bereaved family and help translate so they would be more comfortable when we went to the funeral home the next day.

That evening, my husband and I met the wife of one of the deceased, and the daughter who was driving during the accident. I gave them a cake I'd baked. There were others there, but introductions were incomplete. Despite their unspeakable misfortune, everyone seemed oddly composed. There were no tears, no asking *why*. Occasionally, I thought the daughter — who was bruised and swollen — was going to cry, but she never did. I couldn't decide which was worse, grieving or watching the heartbroken quiver in their determination to keep from falling apart. When handed a large, blurry photograph of the deceased, I was unsure what to say. I smiled and nodded. We attempted several conversations about paying for services, whether the family wanted a cremation, what to do with the ashes, and whether a viewing was possible based on the body's condition. None of it made sense. With Sonny's broken English, strong accent, and a complicated context, communicating was confusing. My husband and I listened hard, to no avail. Sonny was having a similar challenge, since the family spoke a different dialect. At one point after speaking with the family, he shook his head and said, "I have no idea what they are saying."

Mercy was the word that came to mind at that moment. These refugees, experiencing the profound loss of their patriarch, livelihood, and their life as they knew it, were at our mercy in what was surely one of their darkest hours. The language barrier and their loss made them vulnerable, and the magnitude of it felt enormous to me.

When we left, a lively and playful eight-year-old boy asked Sonny, "Hey, are you going to see my dad now?" Sonny said, "Nah," shaking his head and shutting the boy on the other side of the door. I asked if the boy knew his father had died. My heart sank as Sonny told me the boy thought his dad was in the hospital. *He didn't know.* The statement sounded like another question as it resonated in my mind. Finalizing the funeral arrangements with the mother and daughter the next day involved more questions than seemed possible to answer, but they paled in comparison to one question: *Why* do tragedies like this happen? It's easy to misconstrue death as the ultimate defeat. Yet, I believe that in death we will be

> *"And everyone who lives and believes in me will never die." (John 11:26)*

amazed at the mystery revealed to us. We will finally understand how our end is really our beginning, and how suffering helped bring us to salvation. The only thing left to question will be why we questioned at all.

OUT OF THE ASHES

I was almost eight months pregnant with my first child on 9/11. My body was full with the promise of life, and the sky was falling. Thinking of all the service members who have died since then, I wanted to teach my children about the sacrifices that have made their lives possible. We volunteered with Operation USO Care Package, putting together small comforts to send overseas. We wrote notes to include in the packages that we stuffed with razors, toilet paper, toiletry kits, peanuts, beef jerky, and coffee. My sons included words such as *brave, kind,* and *helpful* on their notes, and, like mine, each one began with *thank you.* Thinking of the uncomfortable conditions service personnel endure, the families they leave behind, and the fellow soldiers they watched die, *thank you* seems inadequate.

It was unbearably hot, and my boys were starting to look

faded, so we broke for lunch. On the way to the restaurant, we talked about the sacrifices made by those who serve. Interrupting me, my oldest son asked, "Are you going to cry?" I laughed. As much as we had sweated in the sizzling heat, I don't think I could have mustered a single tear. Besides, I didn't feel sad — just grateful to those who ensure our freedom. After lunch, we returned to the cadence of stuffing care packages with military precision. I don't know why my children didn't complain, or ask how much longer, or act like the silly boys they so often are, but we worked in silence. Maybe it was in reverence to the soldiers who protect our freedom by willingly sacrificing their lives.

> *"The last enemy to be destroyed is death."*
>
> *(1 Corinthians 15:26)*

I still recall the urgency I felt to bring my son into a world that suddenly seemed fragile, and all these years later I celebrate the life made possible by their sacrifices. *No tears, just gratitude.* While the destruction from 9/11 was devastating, it was also a resurrection for our nation. A new commitment to patriotism rose like a phoenix out of the ashes on that pivotal day. We buried our dead with sorrow and dignity, but we also rose up from the apathy and complacency that is easy to fall prey to. The horror of 9/11 wounded the heart of this country in an unprecedented way, but those terrorists were anything but victorious. We did not turn toward the same kind of evil. Instead, we turned toward one another: to comfort, heal, and begin again. While there are also those who celebrated the crucifixion of the Lord, they too were not victorious. Within three days, Jesus rose from the dead. It is the ultimate joy of our faith to know that death is but a gateway to eternal life.

ANGEL OF DEATH

When Teresa died, I'd been at the hospital all day trying to help her family. After everyone left, I stayed to pray over her lifeless body with the priest and deacon. It was a long, horrible day. I dreaded the many phone calls I still had to make to share the devastating news. I had already said "I'm sorry" to too many people. It felt like the most apologetic day of my life. I came home depleted and was surprised to see a Styrofoam cooler on my dining room table, brought by my friend Julie Anna. On top of it was a bouquet of long-stemmed sunflowers that suggested the return of sunny days. Inside was dinner for my family. Overcome with humility at the mercy extended to me, I sobbed. It wasn't just a meal she gave, but the mercy to pause and recognize that my own pain mattered. Her kindness acknowledged my own overwhelming grief. Marked on top of the cooler were two words: *Mercy Matters.*

The mercy we share always matters. Acts of compassion extended through a sympathy card, hot meal, prayers, hand-holding, or the logistics of funeral arrangements offer profound comfort to the bereaved. Sometimes just being present is the work of mercy that matters most. Sprouting from the death of winter into the hope of spring is the fragile bloom of memories that remain in our hearts, dulling the thorny sting of loss. Stand in witness to those memories.

GLORY, GLORY, HALLELUJAH

Faith is our greatest weapon in the battle over grief. By remembering that all things work together for the glory of God, trusting that our loved ones are resting in the merciful arms of our Savior, and honoring the dignity of life through memorializing our dead, we can rejoice despite the pain of grief. Burying the dead offers the opportunity to reconcile our loss through the merits of Jesus' resurrection, which transformed sadness into celebration.

One of my favorite Church celebrations is All Saints' Day. For years I have attended the school Mass where children from ages four to fourteen dress as their favorite saint and process into the church to the lively, up-tempo music of "When the Saints Go Marching In." The joy is palpable. It's a recognition of our individual call to be saints and the jubilation that awaits. While we live in a world where we believe only what we see, hear, and touch, or what has been validated by science or an Amazon review, an eternity with God awaits. While the promise of heaven can't be substantiated by the world's standards, it is authenticated in the love we share during our time on earth. Love that marches to its own tune. "Oh Lord, I want to be in that number, when the saints go marching in."

> "But, as it is written,
>
> 'What no eye has seen,
>
> nor ear heard, nor the
>
> human heart conceived,
>
> what God has prepared
>
> for those who love him.'"
>
> (1 Corinthians 2:9)

MERCY WORKS: TRY IT

Saint John Chrysostom said, "Let us not hesitate to help those who have died and to offer our prayers for them." Let us put our prayers into action as we bury the dead with honor and compassion.

- *In your home*: Whether from the loss of a loved one or the grief of never feeling good enough, make your home a place for healing. Consider starting a notebook to communicate with your children, allowing them to write feelings they may feel too uncomfortable to share face to face. Teach your children to attend funerals, send sympathy cards, and make meals for the bereaved. Give everyone space to grieve, and respect that we all mourn differently. Create "rules" for grieving where no feelings are bad, crying and anger are acceptable, and trusting God is encouraged. Share your end-of-life wishes with your spouse, making sure your will and other legal documents are in order. Leave a legacy of faith and love that will comfort and bring strength to your family after you have passed. *Make happy memories.*

- *In your community*: Support hospice or other end-of-life organizations. Volunteer at a camp for bereaved children. Visit the dying, especially those in nursing homes or hospitals where they may be alone. Honor our fallen military by showing reverence to the flag and supporting military families. Help tidy a cemetery or graves in disrepair. Offer both practical and spiritual help. Look after children, do laundry, run errands, help plan funeral services, pray, send Mass cards, and make memorial donations. Start a fundraiser, plant a tree, or fund a scholarship. Keep the deceased alive by emulating what you loved most about them. *Remember.*

- *In your personal relationship with God*: Ask God to turn your grief into healing. Unite yourself to his suffering. Remember how Jesus wept for his friend Lazarus. Celebrate and offer gratitude for the joy of Jesus' resurrection and recognize that through his mercy, his risen life is available to each of us. Receive

the risen Jesus in the Eucharist as often as possible.
Start anew by making a good confession and letting
go of what buries you. Rise up to be who he created
you to be. *Live fully.*

REFLECTION QUESTIONS

When you think about your departed loved ones, what do you
remember most about them? Which of those memories sustain
you and which can you bring to God and ask him to turn your
grief to healing?

What Scripture verses offer you hope in your grief? Who in your
life might need you to share that hope today?

Thinking beyond the immediacy of death, what are some ways
that can help the bereaved in the months and years following
their loss?

PRAYER

Dear Jesus, help me not to fear death for myself or those I love.
Comfort me during times of grief and help me to comfort others
who are overwhelmed with the loss of a loved one. Give me the
strength and devotion to serve you and others so that on the
Alleluia day of my death, I can become a saint and rejoice for
eternity with you in heaven.

Part Two

The Spiritual Works of Mercy

8
Admonish the Sinner

*"I know that the Lord is always on the side of the
right; but it is my constant anxiety and prayer that
I and this nation may be on the Lord's side."*
Abraham Lincoln

Do you ever just want to tell someone they're messing up? *"Hey, you! There is a train coming towards you at one hundred miles per hour, so you may want to get off the tracks?"* Presumably, we'd all say something if someone was in physical danger, but when it comes to spiritual threats, it's easy to stay quiet. The world's prevailing message is we can do whatever we like as long as it doesn't hurt anyone else. This mentality might not be so absurd, if it were possible. If we all lived in bubbles and our

107

actions didn't affect or influence others, then maybe this idea would float. Engaging in self-sabotaging behavior can cost jobs, destroy marriages, enable addicts, bury someone in debt, ruin friendships, and even take a life. With so much at stake, it seems we wouldn't be so reticent to admonish our neighbor. But most of us avoid difficult conversations because we worry about being perceived as judgmental or as overstepping. Yet this is the hard work of love and one of the most beautiful acts of love we can do for one another. The people in my life, to whom I am most indebted, most loyal, and for whom I am most grateful, are those who have risked having hard conversations with me. They came into my lane, got into my business, and pointed out the risks and consequences that went beyond the bubble of my life. I know it all sounds terribly dramatic, or at least just terrible, but when you really think about your own life, you have either been lucky enough to have someone yank you off the track or unfortunate enough that you wished someone had.

We live in a world where admonishment is equated with intolerance, instead of seen as an act of love. At the same time, conflict has become a country pastime. From identity politics to gender identity, social media rants to societal outrage, and protests to parodies, recrimination of our neighbor has become a source of entertainment, polarization, and finger-pointing. Instead of adhering to the truth, society urges us to insist on being right and reduces loving our neighbor to mean loving those most like us. But admonishing sinners is meant to be loving, not loathsome. Our culture today discourages us from correcting those who act against God's law. While we seek to help people escape from things that are hurtful to themselves and others, we can often be considered judgmental instead of judicious. As a result, many of us avoid our Christian call to offer gentle correction that could save our neighbor from the inevitable pain of sin.

Conversely, when it comes to admonishing ourselves, we

tend to get swept away in self-criticism. We may be reluctant to correct our neighbor, but we give our inner critic free reign, spewing self-destructive thoughts that are not rooted in the truth of God's love but in the lies of the devil. This self-condemnation leaves us feeling inadequate, discouraged, and distracted from the fundamental message that God is madly in love with each of us. To practice this important work of mercy, you might begin by rejecting the lies of your inner critic. Instead, listen for the life-giving correction of the Holy Spirit that lifts you up and gives you strength to do better. When you treat yourself with the same patience that God has with

> *"My friends, if anyone is detected in a transgression, you who have received the Spirit should restore such a one in a spirit of gentleness."*
>
> *(Galatians 6:1)*

you, it helps stop the spiral of condemnation. We are not perfect or beyond reproach, but there is a difference between self-criticism and correcting sinful behavior. The better you get at rejecting your inner critic, the easier it becomes to lovingly admonish others when a situation occurs.

By accepting the truth of our imperfections, our own need for mercy, and the grace God gives us to fill the gaps of our iniquities, we're less resistant to correction of ourselves and others. The work of mercy to admonish sinners has nothing to do with criticism, belittling, or humiliating our neighbor. It's an act done in the spirit of love, which sees the good in ourselves and others and seeks to draw it out.

SLIPPERY SLOPE

My fourth-grade teacher used to say M.Y.O.B., an acronym for "mind your own business." There are certainly times in life when her directive is wise. By minding our own business, we avoid temptations to judge, gossip, or manipulate situations. However, when it comes to admonishing sinners, M.Y.O.B. can be terrible advice, getting you in more trouble than detention. It becomes a disservice to our neighbor who we have been commanded to love. The truth is everyone's business, because it comes from God. Patrick Henry, one of our country's founding fathers, spoke to the timelessness of genuine truth when he said, "The eternal difference between right and wrong does not fluctuate. It is immutable." The key to admonishing others correctly is to act in accordance with the wisdom of God's truth, not the whims of humankind. Words such as *freedom, tolerance*, and *equality* have been exploited to mean that everyone should do what they want. Speaking against this mentality is heresy in today's world. It comes off as an unfair imposition of values, rather than what it is: encouragement to act like Christ. Even for those of us who are committed to living like Jesus, being told we have done something wrong usually makes us feel defensive and angry. That's why it's always important to make admonishments gently and privately, and when you are the one being called out to accept correction with openness and grace.

The world likes to make heroes out of sports icons, celebrities, and fairy tale royalty, but the true heroes are those who understand the sacrificial nature of love that sometimes requires hard conversations. Genuine love takes on the challenge of correction. It understands that love is not synonymous with yes. It is more than affirmation. It is accountability for the sake of salvation. Genuine heroes fight a battle over the evils of apathy, ignorance, and selfishness. True heroism has nothing to do with caving in, turning a blind eye, or shrugging things off. Saint Augustine said, "Right is right even if no one is doing it; wrong is wrong even if everyone is doing it." The difference between right and wrong isn't about trends; it's about the love of our neighbor, which God has commanded is every bit our business.

"Let the word of Christ dwell in you richly; teach and admonish one another in all wisdom."

(Colossians 3:16)

WRONG DIRECTION

If I know anything, it's the spiral of self-admonishment. It's astonishing how many different ways there are to communicate inadequacy to yourself. Every part of my identity as a mother, wife, daughter, Christian, friend, and employee was evaluated by the stringent parameters I set. *Did I do enough? Was I kind enough? Will I ever be enough?* If you have ever experienced this, you know what a miserable way it is to live. When you feel unworthy, you are more likely to believe the devil's lies, the litany of *shoulds*, and the criticisms that overshadow Christ's teachings about your inherent value. There's a difference between listening to the wisdom of your conscience and the self-recrimination derived from measuring your value by the world's standards. The first keeps us from sin, while the other instills inadequacy, leaving us vulnerable to sin.

By focusing on the busyness of *better, next,* and *more,* I stopped considering what is and always will be — a God whose love and providence is unconditional, unending, and unsolicited. Mercy gave me the motivation to stop emphasizing the worldly and pay more attention to the worthwhile. It was permission to let go of the perfect and find grace in imperfection. It was possibilities made endless through the merits of forgiveness, the boundless pursuit of compassion, and the insurmountable power of love. Not in the span of a day or even a year, but in incremental shifts and small, seemingly insignificant moments of grace, I realized that however well-intentioned my resolutions were, they were feeding a mindset of unworthiness. Instead, I began to consider the threshold of unconditional love that is the basis of Christianity. I tried to wrap my head around the enormous truth of being loved right where I am, and I started to question the worldly motivations that once ruled me.

Being merciful to yourself requires patience and awareness. Mercy is less of a resolution and more of a refuge. It's a remarkable source of empowerment that helps us release the past so that we are grounded in the present. I've achieved more through mercy than I ever did following even the most stringent of rules. Moreover, I love the freedom that being loved and enough by an

> *"My brothers and sisters, if any one among you wanders from the truth and is brought back by another, you should know that whoever brings back a sinner from wandering will save the sinner's soul from death and will cover a multitude of sins." (James 5:19–20)*

ever-generous God gives me to do *more* — not in terms of mankind's measurements, but as his will manifests in my life. With God's mercy on your side, every moment can be a new beginning — a resolution based not on the critique of rule-following, but on the gentle ruler of your heart.

A MATCH MADE IN HEAVEN

It's odd that we wear such fine attire on our wedding day when marriage is so messy. It seems like it would be smarter to wear body armor or at least a sturdy raincoat to better prepare us. Yet, the bride and groom don lace and bow ties, veils and patent leather, pearls and cuff links, willingly pledging themselves to each other until death. It's all so genteel that it's hard to imagine the years that follow are anything other than champagne and roses. Yet we come with pasts, preferences, and a penchant to think we are right. Part of our vocation in marriage is helping our spouse become a better Christian. Sometimes, this requires gentle admonishment in the spirit of love. We start out thinking marriage is going to be a gentle dance like the carefully choreographed one we perform on our wedding day. Yet, inevitably there are missteps, clumsy moves, and moments when we or our partner lets go instead of holding tight, requiring us to have hard conversations. Perhaps the issue is overspending, parental disagreements, substance abuse, distractions from making God the center of your home, or infidelity.

I was teaching children's liturgy one Sunday, and the readings were about marriage. Following the format of that week's lesson, I asked the class to share what it feels like to be left out, ignored, and lonely. One little girl described it as not being seen. Her answer rings particularly true in the Sacrament of Matrimony. It's important in marriage to be *seen*, not only as we are, but in the fullness of what we can become when we live in accordance with God's laws. Marriage is not just about being accepted in as-is condition like some defective discounted merchandise. The sacrament is about helping your spouse become a better person by pointing out sinful behavior and encouraging them to eliminate it.

In marriage, we have made a commitment with the entirety of our earthly lives, but our call from God extends to the eternal. The most important thing we can do for our spouse is help them get to heaven by speaking truth with gentleness. No one wants to be considered hypocritical, intolerant, or judgmental, but the truth is we all fall down. By understanding and accepting the need for admonishment ourselves, we can admonish our spouse without it feeling heavy or laden with judgment. It's not about counting mistakes but considering gentle admonishment as one of the countless ways you show love for your spouse.

Perhaps the reason we don't wear armor on our wedding day is that marriage isn't meant to be perceived as impenetrable. Like everything in this world, it's delicate, fragile, and vulnerable to sin. Having someone love you enough to look underneath the veil of your shortcomings to help you see who you can become in Christ may be the closest thing there is to a match made in heaven.

THE GOOD FIGHT

Perhaps a better way to look at admonishment is encouragement. Encouragement says, "I've got your back," "I know you can do better," "I care too much about you to say nothing," or "Your actions are going to hurt you, and I want to spare you that pain." Genuine encouragement isn't just politeness; it's a sincere sentiment that conveys worth. "I see you." "I support you." "I believe in you." Encouragement gives us the strength to keep going, to believe in ourselves, and to withstand the temptation of sin. We live in a busy world. Too often we don't realize the impact we have on others.

A few gentle words of admonishment can make a difference. We may never know the extent to which our simple pause to help someone back on the right path provides the impetus needed to change his or her direction. Encouragement fights sin with compassion, not conflict. It's the mercy of mentoring that reminds someone of whom God meant him or her to be.

"If your brother sins against you, go and tell him his fault, between you and him alone. If he listens to you, you have gained your brother."

(Matthew 18:15, ESV)

Admonishing sinners is acting with the integrity of a true Christian. It strengthens our resolve to follow God's commandments and examine our own consciences to ensure we are not guilty of hypocrisy before speaking out. As Martin Luther King Jr. warned, "A man dies when he refuses to stand up for that which is right. A man dies when he refuses to stand up for justice. A man dies when he refuses to stand for that which is true." Admonishing someone who is caught in the trap of sin provides a gentle reminder of God's truth and can offer a spiritual lifeline to anyone dying of sin.

NO REGRETS
Our world markets happiness as doing what we like. Yet we see that this can't be true. Living for ourselves alone has resulted in the increasingly divided world we live in now. We are not meant to be fragmented, broken apart from one another like shards of glass ready to pierce. It goes against human and divine na-

> *"Therefore encourage one another and build up each other, as indeed you are doing."*
>
> *(1 Thessalonians 5:11)*

ture. God wants you to be happy, but the happiness he offers also makes you whole. He wants you to love with your whole heart, soul, and mind. He wants you to intentionally consider others in all that you do. This requires the humility of sacrifice. To live only for oneself when we were created to love others goes against our nature. We were made to love, nurture, protect, and care for one another. Only through this can we be whole — and only then will the world be whole. Doing what we were created to do requires sacrifice, obedience, and selflessness, all of which can be a hard sell when competing against the deities of today. The messages of here and now can consume us; they carry a sense of self-inflated significance that distracts us from the everlasting. Our world is obsessed with temporary gratification and goal-seeking. With God there is only one goal: salvation. By admonishing sinners, we lovingly remind ourselves and others of this call.

MERCY WORKS: TRY IT

"All scripture is inspired by God and profitable for teaching, for reproof, for correction, and for training in righteousness, so that everyone who belongs to God may be proficient, equipped for every good work" (2 Tm 3:16–17). Using the truth of Scripture, let's equip others to do the good works they were created for by admonishing sinners when it's appropriate — while being prepared to receive admonishment ourselves.

- *In your home*: Ask your children to look into their own hearts and consider the ways they may be failing God. Teach them the difference between tattling and helping others stay on the right path. Practice admonishment by role-playing different scenarios and showing alternate approaches for the same situation. Demonstrate the difference between being confrontational and compassionate. Set an example of accepting admonishments with grace and point out ways that others can too by brainstorming examples. Encourage your children to speak up for those who can't advocate for themselves. Teach them to pray for others and do works of mercy for the conversion of those trapped in the bondage of sin. One of the best things we can do for our spouse is help them become better Christians. Agree to be open to each other's suggestions for improvement. Together, decide how you will approach admonishing situations with each other. Respect the guidelines you set. Encourage family members by telling them at least three things each day that you like about them. Be an example.

- *In your community*: Reframe admonishment from judgment to encouragement that leads to true conversion. Admonish privately and in the spirit of love. Express concern, not judgment (after all, it's hard to be angry at someone who is worried about you). Speak against injustice, whether it is against the oppressed, the poor, the unborn, the elderly, or the imprisoned. This can be through protesting, writing to politicians or penning letters to the editor, supporting fundraisers, and talking to friends and coworkers. Share your own conversion story. The details don't have to be similar for it to be effective. We can all fall prey to sin. Likewise, we can all pray for and help one another avoid it.

- *In your personal relationship with God*: Examine your own heart. How is sin keeping you from God? What are some practical ways you can avoid these temptations? Go to confession frequently. Make amends to God through acts of kindness. Ask God to help you receive admonishment with grace by not getting defensive or angry. Make a commitment to consider admonishment from others as an act of love. Stop the spiral of self-admonishments that bind you. Recognize them for what they are: lies of the devil. Believe the beautiful truth that is in Scripture: "This is how we know what love is: Jesus Christ laid down his life for us. And we ought to lay down our lives for our brothers and sisters" (1 Jn 3:16, NIV).

REFLECTION QUESTIONS

Have you ever regretted not admonishing someone for something they were doing that would hurt themselves or others? Do you think you would do anything different now?

Does receiving admonishment make you feel defensive? How can you accept criticism as a chance to convert away from sin?

How can you become more aware of self-admonishment and how can you use God's mercy to obliterate those destructive thought patterns?

PRAYER

Dear Jesus, please give me the wisdom to know when to intervene in someone's life and the gentle words of humility to do so in a way that is encouraging and enlightening. Give me the strength to avoid judging others. Grant me the humility to receive correction when I am the one being admonished. Help me to realize the value and dignity of every human life and treat each person as my brother or sister in Christ. Banish Satan's evil lies from my head so I can listen to the love you speak in my heart. I pray this in your name.

9
Instruct the Ignorant

*"I did then what I knew how to do. Now
that I know better, I do better."*

Maya Angelou

My newborn son slept in such quick spurts that he was like a
jack-in-the-box on autopilot. As soon as we thought he was
down, *boing!* he was awake again. My body ached with exhaustion, my weary eyes twitched, and the static that fogged my brain
buzzed like a poltergeist. I was so tired I almost ate the stub of
his umbilical cord that unbeknownst to me had fallen off near
the bag of Craisins I kept in the bed to snack on during late
night nursing sessions. (I have had an aversion to Craisins ever
since.) Frantically, I thumbed through different parenting books

desperate to find the chapter that taught "Sleep 101." No matter how many books I read or techniques I employed, I couldn't get my son on a nursing schedule, sleep schedule, or mama-real-ly-needs-a-shower schedule.

Likewise, right before my first son became a teenager, I begged a friend — in the name of all that is holy, all that is sane, and all that is merciful — to lend me every parenting book she owned. After seeing the stack piled in my office, my younger son asked why I had so many teenager books. Before I could respond, he prophetically answered his own question, "Oh yeah, it's going to be a long seven years ... " The work of mercy that most embodies parenting is to instruct the ignorant. However, it took me a while to figure out that maybe it was me, the mama, who needed the most instruction.

Whether you are a parent or not, instructing the ignorant is a powerful act of love. We are all called to be teachers, and of all the things you teach others in life, your faith is most important. Wherever you are on your own faith journey, you have some-thing to teach through your Christian example, your knowledge of Scripture, your devotion to the saints, the eloquence of your communal prayers, or any of the other multitude of ways that we express our faith. You don't need degrees in theology or disser-tations on discipleship to qualify as a teacher. Society touts that without proper (and costly) credentials, we don't have what it takes to instruct others. It wants the research, metrics, and facts to substantiate faith. But this fails to understand that faith is about a relationship with God first and foremost. It's impossible to share the Good News of Christ if we don't know him, what he lived, and why he died. The better you know God, the more you can teach others while strengthening your own faith.

KNOWLEDGE IS POWER

In a reporting class I took in college, if a student's article had any factual errors, the instructor automatically took fifty points off their grade. It didn't matter how insignificant the mistake was, it resulted in an inevitable failure on the assignment. Fact checking was more important than your lead, punctuation, or your inverted pyramid. The paramount significance of truth in news reporting was underscored.

Today a spiritual battle for the truth is raging. The maxim "knowledge is power" applies to everyone, from do-it-your-selfers to delegators. Information is the premier commodity in today's economy. Despite unprecedented access to data, ignorance and inundation prevail. Sources can be biased and unreliable. News outlets, social media, and email bombard us. We are so data-saturated we stop discerning sources and rely on soundbites to form opinions. Our society views truth as relative, not absolute — spliced and manipulated based on perceptions and polarizations of ideologies and agendas. As Saint Toribio wisely reminds us, "Christ said, 'I am the truth'; he did not say 'I am the custom.'" Universal truths exist, and we need to know, live, and speak them.

> *"Stand therefore, and fasten the belt of truth around your waist, and put on the breastplate of righteousness."*
>
> *(Ephesians 6:14)*

By armoring ourselves with the truth of our faith we can become teachers of it. We can do this by attending retreats, listening to speakers, reading religious books, participating in Bible studies, and studying the saints. Armored with the truth of God, discernment becomes clear, and the world's falsehoods are more easily identified and dismissed. God's truth doesn't vacillate, waver, or become fictionalized regardless of situations or circumstances. That's a fact, a truth that gives a whole new meaning to making the grade, if we live by it.

MERCY MANIFESTO

When my son became a teenager, I wrote a sort of manifesto for the teen years. I clicked away at the computer doing the holy work of creating the instruction manual for parenting that I wished I had. It read like a contract, with caveats and consequences included for clarity. It featured equations for various if/then scenarios and clearly proved my naiveté is boundless. Still, it was *beautiful.* It had italics and bullet points and fancy words such as *parameters, privileges, outlined,* and *occasionally.* I signed it, not with the slang *Yo' mama,* but with the sincere, sweet *your mama* that is so obviously *me.* Perhaps it was the lull of the dishwasher that my son ran without my asking, but I was uncannily calm as we spoke, the two-page, single-spaced manifesto at my side. I didn't boss or dictate. I simply made my expectations clear, distilling the manifesto's pages into a few concise sentences that wouldn't warrant any fancy punctuation if they were written. After we kissed goodnight, I sat alone with the manifesto, a mostly read parenting book, and familiar thoughts on how nothing about parenting goes to plan. As beautiful as it was, the manifesto I wrote paled in comparison to the innate beauty of my son, who deserved more than strategies, systems, and contrived solutions. He merited the mercy of a mother who didn't treat him as something to conquer but someone to contour through the patience of love. I folded the manifesto and threw it in the trash.

Parenting may be more gut-wrenching than glorious, but it is no doubt the most holy work you will do. The *Catechism of the Catholic Church* tells us that "parents have the first responsibility for the education of their children" (2223). Demonstrating mercy while teaching your children about their faith, the world, and the imminent need for service will help them model compassion for others. By not demanding perfection of yourself or other parents, you can emulate mercy. Every mother I know sacrifices, struggles, and feels alone, unsure, and terrified of screwing up the sacred gift of life. Yet they have strength to press on, rise to the challenge, love through hardship, and feel immense gratitude for the children with whom they've been entrusted.

Parenting isn't about your capacity to follow instructions in a book, or to implement the logistics of a schedule. It's not about doing everything right or well or worthy of a Pinterest board. Parenting is about modeling the holy family, trusting in the mercy of God and the grace that fills the gaps. Sometimes it's allowing ourselves the mercy to feel gratitude for wherever we are on our parenting journeys — even if you're like me and still desperate for hacks to

> *"Train children in the right way, / and when old, they will not stray."*
> *(Proverbs 22:6)*

get teenage boys to sleep. There aren't enough words in all the languages of the world to write what I have learned from my children, even though I'm the one who is supposed to be the teacher. Yet it's okay that parents don't have all the answers. If you instill in them a genuine love and reverence for God, your children will be equipped not only to navigate the secular world, but to minister to it. Sometimes I lie in bed late at night thinking about my boys — how proud I am of who they are and who they are becoming. It's kind of nice to give myself that mercy. Besides, I am going to be awake anyway.

TRY, TRY AGAIN

One of the things that made me feel most qualified to do works of mercy and share my experiences with others was that I was completely unqualified. I don't have a degree in theology. I can't recite Scripture or remember all of the gifts of the Holy Spirit. I can't even begin to tell you all of the things I don't know. Yet my encompassing ignorance motivated me. I knew that if, in my utter ordinariness, I can understand mercy and apply it to my life, my family, and my community, then anyone can. More so, I believe that if we all made an intentional effort to practice mercy in daily life, we would change our own lives and the lives of others. Everything I have learned since came from that willingness to try. It's what motivated me to sign up for a silent retreat where I spent a weekend listening to the deafening noise inside my head. It's what made me drag my girlfriends to a parish retreat where there was more laughter and tears than hormonally seemed possible. It's what made me say yes when I was invited to Bible studies, prayer groups, Christian book clubs, and volunteer efforts in the community. It's what inspired me to teach others about God when I was a confirmation sponsor, taught children's liturgy, or shared my experiences at speaking events. The more I exposed myself to opportunities to learn about God or Catholicism, the more organic it felt. I stopped feeling like an impostor and found a place of belonging alongside other people who cared about cultivating their faith.

We often think where we are in our spiritual journey defines how much we please God, how much he loves us, and how worthy we are of his mercy. Yet God isn't about the perfect but the persistent. He loves our trying. He loves that *we want to* even if we haven't quite done it yet. He loves it when we stay on our spiritual journeys even when we keep taking the wrong path. Too often, we hesitate in our relationships with God because we aren't where we want to be. We get so focused on getting *there* that we forget that we are loved right *here.* Our spiritual journeys aren't meant to be finite. We are all ignorant to some degree. There's always going to be someone who knows more than us, but there's also always going to be something we can teach others despite our perceived deficiencies. What matters isn't how smart we are, but how willing we are to make an effort to know the Lord. We forget the way he delights in our desire for him. Thomas Merton wrote in *The Seven Storey Mountain,* "My Lord God, I have no idea where I am going. ... But I believe my desire to please you does, in fact, please you." Maybe I am still ignorant, but Merton's words make perfect sense to me.

> *"May my teaching drop like the rain, / my speech condense like the dew; / like gentle rain on grass, / like showers on new growth."*
>
> *(Deuteronomy 32:2)*

DO YOUR HOMEWORK

Jesus was the consummate teacher. In the Gospels, Jesus is directly addressed ninety times, and sixty of those were as "teacher." By schooling yourself in Scripture, the *Catechism,* and the nuances of your faith, you can share it in a way that does justice to its promise. You don't have to be a professional teacher in order to do this. We are all responsible for instructing others as an organic part of daily life. By studying our faith, we can experience the joy of empowering others while learning what a gift we've just given ourselves.

When I was in high school my religion teacher, Sister Edith, used the *Star Wars* trilogy to teach about God. At the time, this was light-years over my head. More than a decade later, as the mother of two boys, a barrage of *Star Wars* movies, figures, Legos, lightsabers, Stormtrooper blasters, and bobbleheads invaded our home. Once again, I was forced to watch *Star Wars*. Lots of it. Our family friends, Lynn and Bruce, had two boys the same age as ours, and we saw them often. Lynn was always trying to get Bruce to convert to Catholicism. They had been married for several years, and he was adamant that he wasn't interested. Our children were obsessed with the *Star Wars* movies, and Bruce was a big fan too. I told him about Sister Edith's class and how she used the movies to teach us about our faith. It seemed like after that, our conversations always veered toward God, which I much preferred to talking about the Death Star.

Noticing that Bruce was comfortable discussing his faith with me, Lynn officially appointed me to be in charge of his conversion. While I knew that only the Holy Spirit could do that, I encouraged him to consider Catholicism and continued talking to him about the Faith. Eventually he made the decision to join the Roman Catholic Church and asked me to be his RCIA (Rite of Christian Initiation of Adults) sponsor. We began attending the required classes together every Sunday after Mass, and I was astounded at how my own ignorance of Catholicism felt like it stretched into a galaxy far, far away. As a cradle Catholic, I had been asleep to the rich history of my faith. By choosing me as his sponsor Bruce inadvertently gave me the opportunity to learn about the most important subject in the universe. He may have known less than I did, but because of him I am less ignorant. There's always something we can learn from others, and the best teachers aren't always the most obvious. I still don't get all of the nuance and symbolism Sister Edith taught using those films, but I discovered that I learned the most by being willing to share what little I knew.

Much like students at the culmination of a school year, we will be evaluated at the end of our lives. The rubric that determines the fate of our eternity is contained in the Ten Commandments, Scripture, and in the example of Jesus as a teacher. Instructing the ignorant doesn't require specialized training or degrees; it only requires that you know your faith and model it. Misinformation and ignorance about Catholicism are rampant in our world, for social, personal, and cultural reasons. We fail to practice our faith when we immerse ourselves in a society that prefers the god of more to the God of mercy. In spite of the challenges, we are called to persevere, doing all we can to learn, live, and teach our faith to others. The world's need for Christian instruction is crucial. Through friendship, example, and involvement, you can share your faith by embodying it. This work of mercy gives you an opportunity to study the rich history of the Catholic Church so that

> *"And God has appointed in the church first apostles, second prophets, third teachers."*
>
> *(1 Corinthians 12:28)*

you can share it with others. Besides, an eternity spent with God is worth whatever assignment it takes.

MERCY WORKS: TRY IT

Saint Augustine asked, "Dost thou hold wisdom to be anything other than truth, wherein we behold and embrace the supreme good?" Let us cling to the wisdom of God's truth and embrace the good of instruction on behalf of those we love.

- *In your home*: Instruct your children in life's most

important lesson — their faith. Teach through example. Visibly study your faith in front of your children. Attend a retreat with your spouse. Discuss ways that you can encourage each other's spiritual formation. Participate in Bible studies, discuss what you learn, and brainstorm ways to translate it from text to the age of technology. Make a commitment with your spouse to learn more about your faith — perhaps taking turns in choosing and leading what is studied. Give your children books on the saints, the Catholic Faith, and the Holy Bible. Encourage them to journal as they read, identifying what they like best, exploring what didn't make sense, and discovering what they most want to share with others. Have older kids teach younger siblings about the Faith. Empower them with the truth so they are motivated to share it with peers, especially as they face pressures from the outside world. Do a family Bible study, saint of the week, or watch a religious movie together and discuss it. Pray the Rosary.

- *In your community*: Volunteer to teach religious education in your parish. Mentor at-risk children. Gently teach others about your faith and why you believe what you do. Clarify misconceptions and correct false information. Take opportunities to attend conferences, workshops, and religious studies to enhance your understanding of the Faith. Buy religious books as gifts to encourage others to pursue their spiritual development. Model the joy of our faith so that others will be curious about its redemptive power. Do something nice for a teacher or another parent to show appreciation for their dedication and recognition for their sacrifice.

- *In your personal relationship with God*: Get to know our awesome God! Do a Bible study or daily prayer journal. Read spiritual books. Spend time alone with God and listen to the lessons he's teaching. Challenge yourself to find specific ways to model Jesus and our Blessed Mother. Answer *yes* to God and surrender to his will. Always seek the truth of God's wisdom instead of the world's whims.

REFLECTION QUESTIONS

Thinking back on your life, who has taught you the most about your faith? Why do you think their style of teaching resonated with you?

Even if you don't think of yourself as a teacher or feel knowledgeable enough in the Faith to teach others, can you identify some times in your life where you did teach someone about God or the Catholic Faith?

In what ways can you take advantage of organic opportunities in daily life to teach children, friends, your spouse, and even total strangers about God?

PRAYER

Dear Jesus, please give me the wisdom to always seek your truth. Help me discern what is true in all the information that bombards me. Give me the spirit to joyfully instruct others in the Faith by word and deed. Please have your gracious mother watch over us all — especially the world's children — so that her gentleness and humility will capture hearts, and souls will be set ablaze for you. Amen.

10

Counsel the Doubtful

"Jesus said to him, 'Have you believed because
you have seen me? Blessed are those who have
not seen and yet have come to believe.'"
John 20:29

The world preys on our doubt. Doubt stalks us in the beauty aisle at the drugstore. It assigns standards to meet and encourages comparisons of our insides with the glossy airbrushed outside of someone else. Doubt is a lucrative commodity that leaves us questioning our judgment or compromising our values by succumbing to the bias of businesses who manipulate our uncertainty for gain. Doubt's hunt stalks everything from our parenting to our life's purpose. Doubt tells us no matter what we've done, it's not enough. A mirage of the devil's making, doubt pries us from God's truth and casts us into a pit of lies that snag and splice and undo the holy work of his creation — *but only if we let it*. That's why the work of mercy to counsel the doubtful is so important. It instills the courage to cling to truth, trust in your faith, and hold on to hope, dissolving doubt into dust.

When my son was attending preparation retreats for first holy Communion, he often brought home gifts from the sisters. One gift was a small bag of mustard seeds with a piece of paper attached that read, "For truly I tell you, if you have faith the size of a mustard seed, you will say to this mountain, 'Move from here to there,' and it will move; and nothing will be impossible for you" (Mt 17:19–20). Putting it on the kitchen windowsill, I read it throughout the day. Initially, it didn't mean much. We don't have mountains in Florida, and commanding one to move was beyond my faith threshold. Yet, as days turned into weeks, I continued to read the small slip of paper, and I began to think beyond the words of the verse. I considered how self-imposed limitations inhibit and control us like a puppet master. God wants us to live without the confines of only what we see and touch. He wants us to believe beyond the physical to what we feel and dream and create with the gifts he's given. Yet so often we doubt our gifts. We see them like the mustard seed, a mere speck in a world that spotlights the spectacular. We consider ourselves too ordinary, too busy, or too broken to make a difference. We think the mountain is mightier, while all along it's the mustard seed that has the capacity to grow and transform.

Women seem to have doubt written into our DNA. We question our path, our parenting, our profession, and our purpose. This questioning isn't inherently bad; in many ways this need to solve, strive, and serve is an attribute that helps us discern truth. Questioning only becomes destructive when we seek answers in the wrong places. By focusing on our deficiencies, we forget all that we do well. God made you for a purpose, and it prob- ably doesn't have any-thing to do with what's on Pinterest. Maybe it's not even what you want to be good at. He wants you to love him and others. This doesn't require a compli-cated skill set, and it's not something you can do wrong. God's not put off by your deficiencies. He knows his grace is made perfect in your weakness. By distracting yourself with what you are not, you lose sight of who you are — someone beautiful to God despite your im-perfections. This is the mercy of his love.

> *"Blessed be the God and Father of our Lord Jesus Christ! By his great mercy he has given us a new birth into a living hope through the resurrection of Jesus Christ from the dead."*
> *(1 Peter 1:3)*

There are a lot of things we ask people advice about, but counseling the doubtful is more complicated than helping your girlfriend decide whether or not to buy high-waisted jeans. It's about being willing to help clarify someone's values, navigate personal relationships, deter-mine vocational choices, or decide how to best handle a difficult decision. Most of us have experienced the vulnerability of doubt. The uncertainty, confusion, hesitation, wavering, and fear can be paralyzing. Feeling stuck is one of the worst feelings in the world. We can become so confounded with doubt that we look to the things of this world to satisfy or amplify our worth, which makes

> "He said to them, 'Why are you frightened, and why do doubts arise in your hearts?'"
>
> (Luke 24:38)

the stagnant waters of doubt downright muddy. Counseling the doubtful requires patience to help someone discern what is right or true. It isn't about helping someone decide what will necessarily make them feel happy, but clarifying what God's will is in the situation, recognizing that it offers the only path to genuine contentment.

We can counsel the doubtful by encouraging questions and being open and honest in our responses. Our willingness to sit with someone and listen to their misgivings, fears, and uncertainties gives them a chance to illuminate the sometimes-dark process of decision-making. When we don't have the answers, we can still offer loving reassurance by gathering resources or recommending better-qualified counsel.

This work of mercy helps others see their worth by exposing layers of lies and replacing them with God's truth. It offers a lens that transforms a blur of indecision into clarity. It requires listening to the Holy Spirit, who offers the wisdom of good counsel. Counseling the doubtful does not demand that we have the right answers; it simply requires that we know always to seek Christ as the answer.

DOUBT: THE DEVIL YOU KNOW

I have spent a lot of time with the devil I know. A lot of us do. We are stuck in careers, relationships, routines, and ruts that we long to change, but don't. There is a litany of reasons for this inaction, and they all originate with doubt. Many of us believe the notion that the devil we know is better than the devil we don't. *Maybe* it's because we believe things could always be worse that we are willing to settle for the status quo. *Maybe* it's because change involves ripping off the duct tape that is holding us together, which would let all our broken parts fall free. *Maybe* if we wait just a little bit longer ... *Maybe* can be a terrible place to live in. It's a waiting, a longing, and often, a loathing that has nothing to do with God.

I am tired of the devil I know. I am bored with his same old lies. Baiting us with fear, he snares us into doubting we can do better. By letting fear stop us from pursuing change, we grow stagnant in defeat. Paralyzing inaction that intersects with who God created us to be leaves us at a critical crossroads. Yet I no longer view that unknown path as the scarier one. Maybe it won't lead me to where I want to go. Maybe it will wind away from the comfort that has been my crutch for too long. Maybe it will be lonely, rocky, and wrought with challenges that are an inevitable part of change. But of all the *maybes*, perhaps the most important one to consider is that just *maybe* this new journey will be worth it. Change can be scary, but being smothered under the ash of doubt, paralyzing fear, and the lie that you don't deserve better is what we should really be afraid of.

SEEKING ADVICE

When I was in middle school, I ran an advice column with a classmate. Our last names both began with the letter *C*, so while the national newspapers ran syndicated columns of *Dear Abby* or *Dear Ann Landers*, my Catholic grade school featured *Dear C & C.* Quite honestly, I think we were just as good as Abby and Ann — even if we did make up most of the questions in order to fill the mimeographed page.

I liked the reassurance of advice columns — knowing that someone had answers, that every problem had a tidy, well-written solution, and if we ever needed help, we just had to ask. As I grew into adulthood, I realized it wasn't that simple. Life is more complicated than Abby or Ann ever let on, and full of more occasions for doubt than *C & C* could have known. I learned that help from others could be misguided and some problems don't have prosaic solutions. This was a hard lesson — one that could have easily hardened my heart had I not realized that in all of our questioning and doubt, it's God we ultimately seek. He is unconditionally qualified, the source of peace for the most restless heart. Of course, Jesus doesn't dole out advice in tidy columns of black ink, or answer with the efficiency of email. In fact, he doesn't always consider our difficulties to be real problems at all. Often in our suffering, there may be some lesson he is trying to teach; some letting go he is encouraging; some bigger picture that he is asking us to see. Doling out advice, strategies, and solutions is big business in our world. Yet only through God can our hearts know the peace of doubt's resolve. Only by asking him will we come to know that he is the one true answer encompassing all the answers. By bringing your doubt to the foot of the cross and asking God for guidance, you are assured of the very best counsel.

> *"Do not fear, for I am with you, / do not be afraid, for I am your God; / I will strengthen you, I will help you, / I will uphold you with my victorious right hand."*
>
> *(Isaiah 41:10)*

WHEN IN DOUBT

Counseling a woman considering an abortion allowed me to witness not only doubt's destruction, but also the way hope can deliver us from it. I was volunteering at my local Women's Help Center, and I listened to a woman recount previous abortions through anguished sobs. Her mother had demanded that she get her first abortion. She didn't want to. She didn't think it was right. Yet in our pro-choice world, she didn't feel like she had a choice. Recounting the ordeal of her most recent abortion seemed especially traumatic for her. The procedure had been so painful she couldn't control her screams. Instead of being comforted, she was reprimanded for scaring other patients. She wanted them to stop but felt contractually obligated, since she had signed a paper. She never wanted to experience that emotional or physical pain again. Still, she had a litany of reasons that made pregnancy impractical: unreliable childcare, living below the poverty line, and a minimum-wage working husband. I offered sympathy for her lost babies and the pain she endured. As I explained God's providence and the resources available to help with the logistical and practical issues of parenting, hope ignited in her. She visibly lightened and began talking about keeping her baby. Joyfully, she explained that she suspected she was pregnant because her three-year-old son kept kissing her belly. Tears turning to laughter, we talked about how sweet it would be for him to have a sibling. Hope decimated doubt.

Doubt is a demon that takes lives. Abortion, suicide, eating disorders, domestic violence, and drug use are fueled from doubt. Many of society's problems are rooted in its deception. It causes people to act in unimaginable ways. Skillfully and cunningly, doubt twists us into a dead end of despair, causing us to believe God's hope is unavailable to us. Yet this is never true. Hope is the antithesis of doubt. Hope is of God and makes all things possible. Where doubt destroys, hope gives life. Counseling the doubtful is about restoring hope where doubt has taken over. Sharing hope can dramatically change the world. Its power is from God and can't be defeated by the false deity of doubt.

DOUBTING THOMAS

Sometimes humankind reminds me of a robotic vacuum roaming for crumbs. Setting off definitively in one direction, we hit an obstacle and veer off on a different path. We repeat mistakes and sins much like the miniature vacuum roams the same area oblivious to a logical path. Often, we search for the shortcut, hack, or magic formula to make life easier, and we even do this in our relationship with God. We want to do the minimum: check the boxes of Sunday Mass, grace before meals, and bedtime prayer. We compartmentalize our faith so that it doesn't complicate our messy lives, because following God can be as cumbersome as lugging the big vacuum out of the closet — the one that actually works. We waste energy succumbing to doubt's chase when we know only God can satisfy our innate desire to change, fill our void, and fulfill our purpose. We keep God at arm's length, because it feels too scary to trust him completely. Afraid to surrender, we don't know what he will ask. We doubt we can deliver. Without God at the helm, we wander aimlessly. Maybe eventually we will find that crumb that eludes us, but he wants so much more for us than crumbs.

Like the apostle Thomas, who refused to believe in Jesus' resurrection until he touched the wounds, we let doubt become a barrier to our relationship with God and limit our ability to serve him. We are skeptical that the mercy Jesus offers us through his sacrificial death is available to us. Our misguided culture tells us that our worth is measured by what we accomplish. God doesn't measure our worth by what gets crossed off our to-do list or what attributes the world esteems. So much energy is lost trying to prove we are enough, we are worthy, and we have value. Yet God proved our worth by the same wounds that convinced Thomas to believe in the glory of his resurrection. Any ambiguity you have is made clear by the profound truth that Jesus died for *you* — an act so sacrificial that there can be no doubt of the magnitude of his love. Looking at the cross, we have all the proof we need.

> *"Then he said to Thomas, 'Put your finger here, and see my hands. Reach out your hand and put it in my side. Do not doubt but believe.'"*
>
> *(John 20:27)*

WITHOUT A DOUBT

I grew up in the eighties when war was declared on drugs. The best-known weapon was the three-word slogan, "Just say no." No was encouraged. Like some algebraic equation, a negative turned into a positive. Like all ad campaigns, it ran its course. There was a new decade, new millennium, new drugs, and of course, new wars. "No" is once again true to its definition. It's for the slacker, the one who refuses to lean in. Today, *Yes* has become the world's drug of choice. We are encouraged to go all in, have it all, and do it all. *All for what? At what price?* This twenty-first-century spin blurs priorities, spawning so much of our doubt. Now everything is important. Everything has to be done. It's all-encompassing, egocentric, and exhausting.

Maybe the battle should never have been between yes and no. Perhaps all along it should only have been *know. Know* who should command your heart. *Know* what you stand for. *Know* when to push through and when to pull away. *Know* where you want to go. *Know* why what you do matters.

God knows his plan for us. By pausing long enough to listen to him speaking in the depths of our hearts, we can come to know too. Counseling the doubtful is an opportunity to help others know where God is calling them in their lives. When a friend is struggling in their marriage, with the rebellion of their child, with indecision about how to help their aging parents, or with what to do about a coworker's breach of ethics, you can help them untangle their web of indecision by using your faith to guide them out of the quagmire. Too often, we feel like we don't know. Yet the wisdom of the Holy Spirit is within you. He will guide you with the right words to say or actions to take. Sometimes counseling the doubtful may be as simple as reminding someone of what they already know; other times, it may require brainstorming solutions or offering someone hope. It always involves compassionate and nonjudgmental listening. More than anything, counseling the doubtful is a reminder to help others seek God. By using the tools of adoration, prayer, and Scripture, you can discern through the fog of doubt. *Knowing* God is what gets you there.

> *"For I know the plans*
>
> *I have for you, declares*
>
> *the Lord, plans to*
>
> *prosper you and not to*
>
> *harm you, plans to give*
>
> *you hope and a future."*
>
> *(Jeremiah 29:11, NIV)*

MERCY WORKS: TRY IT

William Shakespeare reminded us that there is good to be won by conquering the enemy of doubt: "Our doubts are traitors, and make us lose the good we oft might win, by fearing to attempt." Let us do good in the name of the Lord by offering counsel to the doubtful.

- *In your home*: Encourage your children to turn to God in times of doubt. Emphasize the certainty of his unconditional love. Discuss ways to be a good friend when others are doubtful. Listen mercifully when your children disclose their doubts. Encourage your spouse to be vulnerable with their doubts. Listen compassionately, offer to pray with them, and remind them of the hope of our faith. Demonstrate how you turn toward God during difficult times and seek friends who listen with the wisdom of the Holy Spirit. Discuss specific ways that God has shown up for you and family members. Study the miracles in the Bible. Share gratitude for the miracles in your life. Approach family relationships with the hope of forgiveness instead of the cynicism of doubt. Believe and encourage one another. Take turns affirming one another. Be sure to praise your children's unique, God-given gifts instead of worldly accomplishments.

- *In your community*: Mentor others. Volunteer to answer phones at a crisis center. Write letters of hope to military personnel stationed overseas. Stand witness to God's hope by volunteering at a food bank, domestic violence shelter, or women's help center. Be kind, open, and approachable so others will feel comfortable seeking your counsel. Listen without judgment and avoid minimizing someone's situation. Offer to pray for a solution. Share a time in your life when you have fallen prey to doubt and ways you were offered help. Remembering that doubt is the devil's work can often prompt us to cling to Christ. Remind those who are struggling of doubt's destruction and hope's promise. Live with the certainty of God's salvation, of hope for better days, and faith in humanity.

• *In your personal relationship with God*: Fill yourself with mercy for others so that you exude Christ's compassion and are patient and willing to offer counsel. Empower yourself with God's hope and refuse to yield to doubt. Receive the sacraments of reconciliation and the holy Eucharist as often as possible to strengthen your faith. Know that your imperfections don't make you unworthy. Your brokenness doesn't define you. Your purpose is not to achieve glory but to encounter it in everlasting life.

REFLECTION QUESTIONS

Where are you struggling with doubt in your life? Who can help you work through this doubt — a trusted friend, a priest, or your spouse? What holds you back from seeking their counsel?

How can you help your spouse, children, and friends become better aware of identifying self-doubt and ways to eliminate it?

Why do you think it's easier to fall prey to destructive thoughts than to have faith and hope in who God created you to be?

PRAYER

O my dear Jesus, doubt consumes so many of your beloved children. It keeps us up at night and steals our peace. Help us draw closer to you so that by knowing you better we can see more clearly. I rejoice in your power that has the strength to move mountains and the gentleness to heal hearts. Fill me with compassion for others and a readiness to serve. Help me to always know who I am and to whom I belong so that I can serve you with an open and humble heart, knowing that no matter how small the deed, the difference is always magnified by your love. Amen.

11

Comfort the Sorrowful

"The LORD is near to the brokenhearted,
and saves the crushed in spirit."

Psalm 34:18

"Jesus wept" (Jn 11:35). It's one of the shortest verses in the Bible, and also one of the most significant. Nothing makes Jesus seem more human or relatable than when he experienced sorrow. Jesus knew grief when his friend Lazarus died. He knew betrayal when Judas gently kissed his cheek. While alone in the Garden of Gethsemane, he experienced anxiety and fear. *He wept.* Compared to his many miracles, his compassion for the suffering, and the love and mercy he preached, it hardly seems like tears would make the movie trailer of his life. Yet Jesus embraced our humanness so fully that he willingly endured the ache and emptiness of sorrow. It's a poignant reminder that in the loneliness of our pain, we are not alone, nor are we meant to suffer alone. We are called to comfort the sorrowful, to bring Jesus' merciful relief to others.

When I was a little girl, I was shy and spoke only when necessary. Once I found my voice, I felt this urgency to use it. In my twenties, I explained to my boss all the reasons I needed to do an assignment. He approved my request, and still, I continued my explanation. Exasperated, he said, "I got it. I already agreed to it." While the poor man badly wanted me to be finished, I continued my monologue until I finally felt satisfied that my point was articulated accurately and entirely. Thankfully, he was patient and good-natured and didn't fire me. Despite my sometimes-prolific wordiness, when it comes to comforting the sorrowful, even I don't always know what to say. Horrible things happen — uncertainty, tragedy, and unspeakable devastation. *What can you say?* But it's not what we say in times of duress that matters. It's that we show up for one another. We don't have to share words to share sorrow.

When my stepfather died, I don't remember a single word anyone said to me beyond "I'm sorry." But I will always remember the generosity of friends who showed up with meals, the kindness of those who took time to come to the funeral or to send a card. I remember the concern that showed in their eyes, the embrace of their hugs, and the squeeze of my hand. You may not know what to say when it comes to comforting the sorrowful, but simply letting someone know you are there for them speaks volumes.

One way to heal our own pain is by practicing works of mercy, because they connect us to God. Comforting the sorrowful is a meaningful way to practice compassion, worship God, and ease your own aching heart. When we focus on others, we aren't as consumed with our own pain. Serving others negates — even dissipates — sorrow. We are less aware of what we lack and more grateful for our capacity to love. We feel more connected to our brothers and sisters in Christ and can more easily see how our journeys intersect. Jesus came to live as one of us.

> *"Blessed are those who mourn, for they will be comforted."*
>
> *(Matthew 5:4)*

He understands suffering. He experienced it. He endured it. Best of all, he rose above it. The wounds of his human experience — betrayal, rejection, loneliness, loss, and fear — are no more, nor are they forgotten. However unique we feel our circumstances are, he can identify with our plight. Jesus wept. He will hold us in his loving and merciful arms as we also weep. It is by personally knowing God's comfort through the mercy of his consolation that we can best give comfort to others who experience sorrow.

CRYING OUT LOUD

A close family friend's teenager called me one day, upset and confused by the inescapable sadness she felt. Of all the accolades this young person has achieved in her short life, it was her brave act of seeking help that I admire most. She trusted me with her pain. Because she did, her parents and pediatrician were able to get her help, and I was blessed by the sacred opportunity to offer comfort. So often, in sadness, we feel alone. Instead of reaching out, we go further inward. Silence becomes its own source of suffering. Sometimes the people closest to us aren't even aware of our sadness. We skillfully hide, discount, and demonize it. All the while we are surrounded by people who love us, are willing to listen, and would gladly offer comfort and wise counsel.

The very act of hiding pain is really idiotic, considering the universality of sorrow. I should know; I practice this idiocy. I even do it in my relationship with God. When I'm hurting and should be leaning into him, I discount my worthiness by thinking he has bigger problems to deal with. Mine, in the whole scheme I compare things to, is trivial. Yet, we are anything but trivial to him. There is no hierarchy to suffering other than the one we assign, often to minimize our pain to avoid its unpleasantness.

When we cry, well-meaning people often ask, "What's *wrong*?" Sadness is perceived as a defect — something to fix or wipe clean with the swipe of a tissue. We tell ourselves being gloomy doesn't solve anything and no one wants to be around a Sad Sally. Most of my life I chastised myself for crying. I considered it a weakness. After all, rarely does the salt-soaked sadness solve anything. Yet there is nothing weak about feeling sorrow. It's a natural part of life, a sign that we are alive spiritually. Besides, crying doesn't always mean you are sad. It can just as easily mean you have been touched by something. Television commercials, school programs, and even sporting events can fill my eyes — an indication that my heart is full, too. Crying is a testament to our tremendous capacity to love.

> *"Jesus wept."*
>
> *(John 11:35)*

SHARING SORROW

Once I was going to lunch with my mom and my boys when I learned that a friend's mother died unexpectedly. I was stunned and momentarily speechless. Tears of sorrow began to spill onto the sidewalk outside the restaurant. I didn't want to cry in front of my children and knew a public lunch was no longer an option, so I headed back to the car to wait for my mom to get takeout when a man stopped and asked if he could talk to me. I was skeptical. I have seen enough *Dateline* and *20/20* to know "Can I talk to you for a minute?" really means *"I would like to chop you up into tiny pieces and put you in my freezer."* Unbeknownst to me, he had seen my reaction to this unexpected death. "I saw how upset you got back there," he said. "Is everything okay? Is there something I can do for you?" While I was touched by his compassion, I didn't know how to answer his question. It made me realize that sometimes comforting the sorrowful is as simple as asking someone what you can do. The encounter made me contemplate what it means to comfort the sorrowful.

After all, I felt horrible that my friend's mom had died. I badly wanted to do something to ease her pain. I hugged her, held her hand, tried to make her laugh, listened, and baked her banana bread. She asked for prayers and I prayed. She asked me for a lawyer to look into possible malpractice by her mother's doctor. I asked my husband, who is an attorney, to find her the best. I even called the lawyer for her because she was overwhelmed. Maybe it's not what you think of as comfort, but it seemed to help.

Not long after that, another friend lost a loved one. She was overwhelmed and asked me to help write the eulogy. I understood the pressure my friend felt. I remember when I was tasked with writing my uncle's eulogy, I was so distracted by my own grief that I didn't think I could do it. Yet, in the end, it was such an honor to comfort my aunt and cousins with my carefully chosen words. There were many ways I could have comforted my friend, but in that situation the most fitting was to help her write her relative's eulogy.

Through these and other experiences, I've learned there are many answers to the seemingly impossible question of how to comfort the sorrowful, whether it's baking, cooking, sending a thoughtful note, planning or organizing, or recommending a helpful book. It's sometimes simply a matter of recognizing we can all do something to show concern. It doesn't have to be big or brilliant, it just requires us to be there.

MISERY LOVES COMPANY

A classmate of my four-year-old nephew kept crying at preschool, so my nephew put his arm around him and asked what was wrong. Through tears, the boy told him he missed his mom. My nephew responded, "We all miss our moms, but we have to be here anyway." With that, the little boy wiped his face, walked up to the teacher and gave her his dirty tissue. (I know it would have been a cleaner story if the boy just put the tissue in the trash.) My nephew's ability to identify with what his friend felt helped his friend to move on.

Regardless of our age, it's a comfort to know we're not alone. So often, in our sadness, loneliness, and lowliness, we feel like the only ones. We can become ashamed of our sorrow, causing us to self-isolate. This can make us feel worse and compounds the shame we feel. Sometimes comforting the sorrowful is as simple as letting someone else know that what they feel is okay. Being reminded that it's normal to feel all of the emotions associated with our sorrow is a great comfort. Talking about things takes the sting out. It eliminates unnecessary shame so you can feel the pain and move on from it.

At the same time, accepting comfort can be difficult. When I unexpectedly received a serious medical diagnosis, friends reached out to show their concern. While I was grateful for their acts of love, even the simple act of listening to a comforting voicemail felt impossible to me. I was having a difficult time accepting the randomness of my situation and dealing with the necessary and immediate issues it involved. I needed time. This is true for all of us when we're sorrowing. Uncomfortable with sadness, we want to hurry through it. Yet, there are no shortcuts with pain. We can't go around it; we don't just get over it; we have to go through it. A one-size-fits-all timeline to grief doesn't exist. There's no checklist that gets it done. There are rarely words that offer genuine comfort. Healing comes when we listen to another's pain or allow someone else to listen to us with compassion. Then, we can surrender our grief to the one God who is big enough to transform it. In the meantime, we can allow others the necessary time to move through their sorrow. This requires patience more than persistence. Pain is never planned. We hardly ever see it coming. Likewise, we have no idea how long it will take to heal.

The source of our sorrow almost always feels complicated. If it were only a matter of logistics, we could solve it. But pain isn't about logistics as much as it is about loss. Our world tells us that anything can be fixed and everything can be bought. It offers myriad ways to distract and numb ourselves. My numbing behavior of choice is shopping. It allows me to confuse having something with having it all together. It offers me an escape from who I am for a chance to discover who I could be. And always, its comfort is hollow and temporary. The reality is that we create more problems for ourselves when we push away our sadness than when we learn to acknowledge, accept, and trust that it will eventually pass.

Comforting others gives us a broader perspective that illuminates

"And after you have suffered for a little while, the God of all grace, who has called you to his eternal glory in Christ, will himself restore, support, strengthen, and establish you."

(1 Peter 5:10)

the lessons of our sorrow while also offering merciful relief. The adage that misery loves company is true when it comes to this important work of mercy. Like Simon did when he helped Jesus carry his cross, we can help others. We can offer a moment of merciful relief as we follow the injunction of Saint Paul to "weep with those who weep" (Rom 12:15).

WEEP FOR JOY

I was picking up throw pillows off my living room floor one morning. (I don't have toddlers, but I have teenagers and there are a multitude of similarities.) I turned around from my pillow pickup and looked out the window to see a pink sky. To my surprise, there was a rose-colored glow on everything: the grass, trees, pavers — all of it. *Pink.* It was beautiful and eerie and made me feel as if the world had stopped and Jesus had come. I kept thinking about the way the sky's color palette changed from ordinary to awesome in what seemed like an instant. It reminded me of our faith journey. Sometimes in our faith walk it feels like we travel alone, especially in sorrow. Then, in God's perfect timing, the darkness recedes. The wait ends. The sound of our tears ceases to be an echo. There is a pink sky.

> *"I have said this to you, so that in me you may have peace. In the world you face persecution. But take courage; I have conquered the world!"*
>
> *(John 16:33)*

There are countless ways we look back at sorrow and see how God intricately wove the tapestry of our journey. Every thread is intentional. Every time we fall down, he lifts us up. His pattern, which sometimes seems haphazard, is always perfect.

During the third week of Advent, we celebrate Gaudete Sunday. *Gaudete* is the Latin word for rejoice. While Advent is a penitential season of expectant waiting and preparation for the coming of Christmas and the second coming of Christ, on Gaudete Sunday we celebrate the joy of God's redemption. With only a week of Advent to go, we pause from our sorrow and rejoice in all that awaits. We light the pink candle on our Advent wreaths. Especially when it comes to times of sorrow, it's important to remember that pink is the color of joy. It's the fulfillment of the promise of our faith that reminds us that our suffering is momentary. Sometimes it's the color of the sky reminding us of the miracles in nature. Sometimes it's the color of our cheeks flushed with joy. Sometimes it's the color that shows up in the love of our neighbor, reminding us that even in sorrow we can experience God's joy.

MERCY WORKS: TRY IT

"Weeping may linger for the night, but joy comes with the morning" (Ps 30:5). Sadness is a normal human experience, but it is temporary; it passes like the night. We can bring joy's light to others by comforting the sorrowful.

- *In your home*: Make your home a place where feelings are not shunned. Encourage your children and spouse to share feelings beyond "fine," "good," and "okay." Identify and discuss healthy coping mechanisms for sadness, such as prayer, exercise, spending time in nature, journaling, creating art, and talking about feelings. When your spouse is sad, make an effort to be thoughtful by making a favorite meal, surprising them with a piece of chocolate, flowers, or whatever else they would consider a treat. Teach your children that comforting the sorrowful doesn't mean you have to know what to say. It's an act of compassion more than conversation. Encourage family members to go on a bike ride or walk with you where they might be more receptive to discussing their feelings. Leave them a note of reassurance or a special Bible verse that speaks to their situation. Help them facilitate a random act of kindness for someone else that will spread joy to their own heart.

- *In your community*: Not everyone who is in pain is walking around with a tear-soaked face and a box of tissues. It's important to treat everyone with gentleness and compassion. Accept that you can't take away someone's pain; part of comforting the sorrowful is giving others necessary time to process grief in their unique way. Notice the people around you and let others know you're there for them. Acknowledge another's pain when you can see that they're sad, or when they tell you about some sorrow they're experiencing. Volunteer as a grief counselor. Join a ministry that helps with bereavement or funeral logistics. Remember significant anniversaries of deaths, birthdays, and other important events. Send a card or offer a Mass. Give the gift of your time and spend time with someone who is hurting.

- *In your personal relationship with God*: Saint Augustine said, "In my deepest wound I saw your glory, and it dazzled me." Bring your pain to the foot of the cross so that you can go from dazed to dazzled. Don't discount or minimize your suffering — offer it to Jesus instead. Ask him to transform it into something that can bring more light into the world's darkness. Sit with God in quiet, through tears, amid the angst and uncertainty. Do not abandon him, and remember that he will never abandon you. Unite yourself to Christ's suffering and crucifixion and remember his joyful resurrection following the sting of death.

REFLECTION QUESTIONS

What comforts you when you feel sorrow?

How has comforting others brought you clarity or offered you a new perspective on life?

Have you ever noticed a tendency to pull away or check out when you're hurting? How can you check in with God instead?

PRAYER

Dear Jesus, console me in my suffering. Help lift the cross of my burdens so that I can know the relief of your mercy. Help me not to turn to the world for comfort or numb my pain with worldly distraction. Teach me what there is to learn from my suffering and how to use it to draw closer to you. Use me to offer light to others who feel sadness. May I be a source of your merciful love amidst their grief. May I remind others that for those who follow you, sorrow will be turned into unimaginable and everlasting joy. This, in your sweet name, I pray.

12

Bear Wrongs Patiently

"You must understand this, my beloved: let everyone
be quick to listen, slow to speak, slow to anger; for
your anger does not produce God's righteousness."

James 1:19–20

The Gospel story of the prodigal son is a parable about a young man who takes his inheritance early, squanders it, and returns home empty-handed to a merciful father who welcomes him back without reprimand or conditions. Instead, the father celebrates.

Sometimes I want to rewrite this story. I don't want the father to run to his son with open arms. I want him to smack his son on the bottom and tell him to apologize to his mother who is worried sick! I identify more with the prodigal son's brother. He stuck around and did his chores and was obedient not because it was easy or desirable, but because he knew it was right. When the prodigal son returns after squandering, schmoozing, and acting all kinds of scandalous, I want to scream, "No fat calf for you!" Yet instead of reprimanding him for his shenanigans, Papa throws a special party to celebrate his homecoming?! I get annoyed just writing about it. In my self-righteousness I'm blinded by the many ways I've been prodigal. I dismiss my waywardness and justify wrongdoing. By comparing myself to far worse, I am complacent about becoming far better. How many times have I been reluctant to admit my transgressions the way the prodigal son did upon his return? The father unconditionally welcomed his return, demonstrating God's merciful patience with each of us.

Likewise, we're asked to be patient with others, even those who are least deserving of it. There are days it feels as if the world is filled with those who make us want to repeatedly bang our head on a concrete floor rather than interact with them. We get infuriated with others — the way they require us to repeat ourselves; relatives who ramble with the same old, tired stories; friends who make a dig about something dear to us; medical staff who abandon us in frigid waiting rooms way past our appointment time. We

"The son said to him, 'Father, I have sinned against heaven and before you; I am no longer worthy to be called your son.'"

(Luke 15:21)

forget they are all beloved children of God. Patience can help us remember.

We are all different — a patchwork of unique experiences, gifts, challenges, histories, and proclivities. Yet often our inclination is to think other people are just like us. We assume they feel the same way about religion, politics, the environment, and high-waisted jeans. When differences arise, we can become impatient and intolerant of other viewpoints. We also become impatient with ourselves when we fail to live up to our own impossible standards. Bearing wrongs patiently is about gaining a fresh perspective as much as it is about practicing patience with those who wrong us (and even with ourselves sometimes). This work of mercy empties us of pride, attachment, and self-importance, while giving us a chance to treat others the way we want to be treated.

TRYING MY PATIENCE

When we toured colleges with our son, I couldn't help but feel impatient with all the "just be you" enthusiasm. After all, most of these schools admit like five new students a year. Extremely competitive colleges with high performing applicants humanize their cut-throat admission policies with a sing-song encouragement to simply be oneself. It's not a bad message in itself, but in a day when diversity has become a means of deliverance, individualism has become an art of self-love. Still, one can only play "*Mirror, Mirror on the Wall*" for so long without becoming utterly bored or an utterly boring narcissist. Loving others has always been where it's at — where we truly feel full, alive, and connected. So, yes, be *you* but don't be all about you.

So much of society's intolerance of one another seems to originate from a sense of entitlement. We believe that our individuality is paramount. We've become impatient with other viewpoints and ideologies. When we let our frustrations dictate our behavior, we lose sight of one another's humanness. We value being right more than being kind. We put determination above someone else's dignity. So insistent on making our voices heard, we forget who those voices hurt.

Many people live in error, and this work of mercy requires patience even when we're affected by their poor decisions. Being patient is a discipline in discipleship: We aren't going to convert others when we fail to act Christ-like. Still, patience isn't just swallowing hard and walking away. Archbishop Fulton Sheen explained, "Patience is not an absence of action; rather it is 'timing,' it waits on the right time to act, for the right principles, and in the right way." We are called to model the patience of Jesus by acting kindly, putting others first, and serving unselfishly.

Patience requires self-surrender for someone else's sake. It's keeping perspective, pausing before speaking, and praying despite feeling compelled to point out. Patience is slowing down when you are antsy to race ahead. It's becoming empowered by mercy instead of overrun by emotion. It's patterning our lives on the lives of the saints, who all started as sinners. The world is a finicky place. God wants us to be who he created us to be, to love fully, and practice mercy joyfully. That journey will look different for each of us, so we need to be patient with those who are on a different path. Being ourselves is a good thing, but it's not the true measure of whether we will be granted admission into the kingdom of God. That measure is

"Better is the end of a thing than its beginning; / the patient in spirit are better than the proud in spirit." (Ecclesiastes 7:8)

always going to be love. And, as Scripture points out, "Love is patient; love is kind" (1 Cor 13:4).

TRANSFORMATION

COVID-19 upended life in unprecedented ways. It was like a global game of freeze tag, where life momentarily stopped while everyone argued over when it would be safe to run again. There were disagreements about what the rules should be and how they would be enforced. The virus became politicized and discussions were polarizing. Some considered mask-wearing to be a form of censorship, while others saw it as a way to save lives. There were plenty of opinions, but patience for others often felt scarce.

At the start of the pandemic, I was a healthy middle-aged woman who spent years as a vegetarian and had a daily exercise routine. Then, in the middle of the lockdown, I randomly had a spontaneous carotid artery dissect, causing a greater than 70 percent blockage. There was no medical reason for my dissection; like so many illogical events of 2020, it just happened. I was basically that cliché of the uber-healthy person who drops dead. Only, by God's grace, I didn't die. For a time though, I was very sick. Because of my condition, I was at a higher risk of having a serious illness from the coronavirus. Warned by my doctor to avoid so much as coughing, strenuous exercise was prohibited. Instead, I began daily walks with two friends.

In an effort to be cautious, I walked on one side of the street while they walked on the other. As strange as it may have been, it was often the part of my day where I felt the most normal. I was so grateful to be out of the house and to have the chance to talk to people that I enjoy. They were incredibly patient with me, too. Whenever they accidently got too close, I would wave my arms, fanning them in the other direction. I'm sure it got old to be constantly waved away, yet instead of being offended by my gesture, they lovingly began calling them my butterfly arms. I know it sounds simple, but it meant the world to me to have people in my life who were willing to accommodate me without making me feel bad. Their patience felt protective. They turned my necessary cocooning into something beautiful through the mercy of their patience.

Whether we believe in mask-wearing or quarantines, vaccines or herd immunity, the new normal or the next wave of infection, school shutdowns or restaurant openings, is insignificant compared to our call to be united in Christ. Living in such turbulent times, self-preservation urges us to only worry about ourselves or those closest to us. Yet, as I scroll through social media and news reports, with their jagged, biting, and bitter words, I can't help but think that we are losing ourselves in this mindset of "me." We are forgetting we have a responsibility to care for our neighbor — the ones we haven't met, the ones whose lives are nothing like ours, and even those who aren't nice people. God has no caveats, and we must not either. Our innate ability to love and care for others is a contagion that thrives even in difficult times. No matter how we perceive our neighbor's point of view, love allows us to see the best in one another. Just as the butterfly eventually emerges from its cocoon, so patience transforms us over time, the more we put it into practice.

THE HIGH ROAD

Bearing wrongs patiently doesn't give anyone the right to take advantage of you. It doesn't mean you don't stand up for yourself or your beliefs. It's important for us to discern when to bear wrongs and when to have boundaries. Wanting to be liked, coupled with the teachings of Christianity about service and loving our neighbor, can often blur our boundaries, leaving us to question how much is enough. It's easy to think that Jesus didn't have a lot of boundaries. During his time on earth, he was out loving everyone — prostitutes, tax collectors, and sinners. His love was boundless and unconditional, his invitation to salvation wide open. *Yet, Jesus had boundaries.* He didn't heal everyone — then nor now. He doesn't always remove our sufferings. He isn't an "anything goes" kind of God.

God never said we need to say *yes* to every request. He didn't tell us that having patience means we need to do everything or try to be everything to everyone. He gave us the tools of the commandments and the teachings in Scripture to help us decide how to be patient with others in a way that isn't self-destructive. Boundaries sometimes blur, often they change, and ideally, they take into consideration the needs of others. Sometimes the best way show love for our neighbor is to walk away, say no, or not now. Christianity requires that we discern for ourselves and the people in our life what to give, sacrifice, and suffer for. We will know how best to practice patience by prayerfully listening to God's will.

> *"Be strong and bold; have no fear or dread of them, because it is the Lord your God who goes with you; he will not fail you or forsake you."*
> *(Deuteronomy 31:6)*

LET IT GO

Do you ever feel like Queen Elsa in the 2013 Disney film *Frozen,* with the phrase "let it go" repeating in your mind? *Let it go* has got to be one of the greatest three-word sentences in the history of ice queens. Conversations with those close to us can sometimes feel like a snowball in the face. The cold grip of truth is that we can't change others. Besides our reaction, we don't get much of a say. Of course, that doesn't mean we don't have much to say — only that we can't control who listens, cares, or jams earbuds in their earholes when we speak.

Patience feels a lot like letting go. Long before Elsa retreated to the ice castle, American theologian Reinhold Niebuhr wrote the Serenity Prayer. He wasn't royalty, didn't have a three-centimeter waist, and couldn't turn people to ice with the flick of his wrist, but he did write a pretty good prayer that inspires patience:

> God, grant me the serenity to accept the things I cannot change,
> courage to change the things I can,
> and the wisdom to know the difference.

Trying to accept what we cannot change often feels like wrestling, wrangling, and wearing ourselves into a state of exhaustion. While acceptance requires patience, it doesn't have to be a frosty experience. Poor Elsa retreated to an ice castle. We can go to God for the serenity of patience. Through the virtue of patience, we can change many things: our perception, attitude, habits, and reactions.

The crux of the Serenity Prayer's message is having the wisdom to know what to accept and what to change. That can feel

"So let us not grow weary in doing what is right, for we will reap at harvest time, if we do not give up."

(Galatians 6:9)

daunting when you feel less like a wise owl and more like you just escaped the cuckoo's nest. Yet, wisdom doesn't have to be hard. Wise people don't overthink things. They know what's right and they act on it. What is your heart telling you? A good rule of thumb is if it's the past, let it go. If change is possible and would make things better, change it. Bearing wrongs patiently isn't as much about wrestling with what infuriates you as making room for Christ's love that bears all things. Letting things go is a way to practice patience while still holding on to the tenets of your faith.

MERCY WORKS: TRY IT

Mahatma Gandhi said, "If patience is worth anything, it must endure to the end of time. And a living faith will last in the midst of the blackest storm." Let us practice patience with an eye toward eternity.

- *In your home*: If what you have to say isn't going to change future behavior, consider letting it go. Picking your battles can be a battle itself when you're impatient, demanding, and unrealistic with expectations. Take deep breaths. Eat a piece of chocolate. Say a Hail Mary. Think before speaking. Give yourself and others the mercy to make mistakes and move on. Ask your spouse how you can show more patience in your relationship. Ask them for more patience with something you are struggling with. Teach your children about patience and validate them for using it. Point out times when they are patient or someone is being patient with them. Use the liturgical calendar as a tool to practice patience. The seasons of Advent, Lent, and Ordinary Time remind us of the cycle and balance of our Christian Faith. Help your kids brainstorm ways to be patient with siblings, friends, and adults. Be patient with your spouse with small things that annoy you. Ask yourself, "Does this really matter?"

- *In your community*: Practice patience as a means of discipleship. Treat everyone with kindness and dignity. Look at others as siblings in Christ and act as Jesus would toward them. Keep pride in perspective and remember to pray, so you can interact with others with the best intentions. Give others the benefit of the doubt. Approach conflict with gentleness. Engage in charitable work that bridges gaps in communication, tears down stereotypes, and seeks to inform others. Avoid the temptation of gossip. When wronged, refrain from gathering a quorum of people who will tell you that you are right. Trust in God's timing and patience and let go of any need to control.

- *In your personal relationship with God*: Ask God to help you surrender to his will, strengthen your trust, and be patient with his timing. Study the lives of saints and try to emulate their example of patience with others. Read Scripture and look for examples of patience. Identify areas where you could be more patient with yourself and others and ask God to cultivate the virtue in all aspects of your life. Offer up aggravating moments as a loving sacrifice to God.

REFLECTION QUESTIONS

How can shifting your perspective toward the eternal transform how you manage daily aggravations? How can you bring this perspective into your daily interactions, not only in person, but also on social media?

In what ways could you show more patience with your spouse, children, and friends?

When you have been shown the mercy of patience, how did it make you feel?

PRAYER

Dear Heavenly Father, please help me to emulate your patience with others. When I feel annoyed and angry, help me recognize the dignity and value of others as fellow children of God. Help me choose love when I want to lash out. Help me to be a witness to all you have taught about love, patience, and mercy. Protect me from pride and my inclination toward justifying my impatience. Be patient with me, dear Lord, as I continue to fall down in efforts to love and serve you. In your great mercy, I pray.

13
Forgive Injuries

"Forgiveness is not an occasional act,
it is a constant attitude."
Martin Luther King Jr.

Valentine's Day and Ash Wednesday fell on the same day only three times in the twentieth century. In this millennium they merged in 2018 and are set to coincide again in 2024 and 2029. There is a certain yin and yang to the secular heart-shaped holiday overlapping with the sacred start of the Lenten season — the commercial hawking of one and the saving grace of the other. Ash Wednesday marks a purposefully non-celebratory season, while Valentine's Day pops with bubbly champagne, decadent desserts, and red roses. The black ash symbolizing death countered with puffy red hearts celebrating love adds an element of realism to the syrupy holiday defined by doilies, hyped-up expectations, and besotted poetry. While true love has more to do with the ashen cross on the forehead, a commonality exists between the days. At the core of each is love.

Lent is the perfect preface to the greatest love story ever told — and *forgiveness* made it possible. God sacrificed his only Son for the forgiveness of our sins. On Ash Wednesday, we are reminded of God's forgiveness, which takes away the stain of our sins. Our hearts, blackened by the wounds of the world, grudges, indifference, neglect, and injustice, can be wiped clean. We are called to seek and share mercy always, not just during the Lenten season. This mercy allows for everything: forgiveness, second chances, redemption, and the glory of new life.

Anyone who has moved past infatuation knows that love is messy. It requires trying again, like Jesus when he fell carrying his cross. Love forgives like Jesus did before he drew his last breath. It's beautiful and redemptive, like Jesus rising from the dead. Compared to shiny, red, heart-shaped balloons, boxes of chocolates, and beautiful bouquets, what God promises is eternal and real. He has the power to heal the dark, wounded places we hide from the world. He forgives our failings and delights in our efforts to know, love, and serve him.

Forgiveness might sound warm and fuzzy, but actually trying to forgive can make us feel as cold as ice. Society espouses paybacks and promises of retribution, while confusing forgiveness with complacency and cowardice. Yet forgiveness requires remarkable strength and perseverance. Anger, resentment, and desire for revenge can enslave us. When we cling to pain, it controls us. Forgiveness is thus an act of empowerment. It's not about minimizing the betrayal of our wounds or letting someone continually treat us poorly. It's not about forgetting. It doesn't mean things don't change, relationships don't end, or that we don't have any more feelings about the situation. It means we choose to let go by acknowledging grievances, feeling our hurt, and making a resolution to have peace with it. Forgiveness also releases the other person from the bonds of our anger. Even when we dislike someone or consider

> *"For if you forgive others their trespasses, your heavenly Father will also forgive you."*
>
> *(Matthew 6:14)*

them untrustworthy, through forgiveness we can still want good things for them. We can still recognize God's love for them. Forgiveness allows someone another chance to get things right. It inspires change and new beginnings.

IN WHAT I HAVE DONE AND IN WHAT I HAVE FAILED TO DO ...

God created us to love one another. There weren't any caveats or exclusions in his command. Somehow along the way, though, we humans continually mess this up. In our society, we have messed this up with people of different races, the disabled, the elderly, the imprisoned, and the unborn. We mess up when we let differences divide us. We mess up when we devalue life of any kind. We mess up when we judge others by what they wear, how they speak, their weight, occupation, what school their children attend, their faith life, marital status, race, income ... and on it spirals. By using secular parameters to define others instead of the unconditional love that God commands, we mess up.

Every day in countless small ways you choose what kind of change to affect in this world. Those choices matter. In the mundanity of your daily routine, you may sometimes forget how much this is so. We can't reconcile our mistakes without first recognizing them. During the Mass, we recite a prayer known as the Confiteor: "I confess to almighty God and to you, my brothers and sisters, that I have greatly sinned in my thoughts and in my words, in what I have done and in what I have failed to do ... " When it comes to social injustice collectively and individually, we have failed our neighbor by both what we have done and what we have failed to do. Yet the great hope of our faith is God's inexhaustible mercy. It can fix any mess.

That people have become angry about indifference and injustice can be a good thing when we channel that anger constructively. It means we want to do better for ourselves, our children, and our brothers and sisters in Christ. It means we are ready for change. Still, anger alone can't get us there. Real change involves the act of forgiveness. Loving our neighbor isn't a sing-song platitude to paste over complicated social issues. It's the way of Christ. It's what we were created to do, and it begins with an awareness of our own failings. The world may want to divide us with labels and judgments, but our greater call is to be catalysts of love and mercy.

I CONFESS

Society loves a good confession. Not sacramental confession, but talk shows, tabloids, tell-all books, and reality television that reveal a provocative secret or betrayal. We binge-watch sordid revelations for entertainment, while we can be reluctant to watch what's in our own hearts. For too many years, I avoided the Sacrament of Confession. A combination of pride, shame, and fear kept my heart darkened with sin. I avoided the sacrament that saves because I was more concerned with saving face. When I finally went, it was awkward, scary, emotional, and inexplicably redeeming. Pope Benedict XVI explained it this way: "Faith in the resurrection of Jesus says that there is a future for every human being; the cry for unending life which is part of the person is indeed answered. God exists: that is the real message of Easter. Anyone who can even begin to grasp what this means also knows what it means to be redeemed."

It's easy to fall into the secular trap of focusing on the righteous things about ourselves: We don't beat our children, we call our mothers, and we return the shopping cart to that little island nowhere near our parked cars. There are a lot of things we do right — *so aren't we good people?* With this as our focus, we minimize the particular ways in which we hurt God. What's one measly sin really going to hurt? Sin is slippery. It starts small, seemingly innocuous, and spreads to places we never considered. But sin doesn't have to be inevitable. You can resolve to do better, avoid its downward slope, and live the holy life that makes your heart whole. While you may fall on occasion, it doesn't have to be the norm. The Sacrament of Confession offers incomparable redemption.

> *"Very truly, I tell you, everyone who commits sin is a slave to sin."*
>
> *(John 8:34)*

Reflecting on our own sinfulness and the inherent flaws of humanity allows us to tap into compassion, making forgiveness of others seem more doable. Reconciliation is a chance to encounter God through the grace of his mercy so we are able to extend that mercy to others.

CLEAN SLATE

When I considered how to forgive, I looked outward to the people in my life who hurt me. I flipped through the catalog of hurts and the people assigned to each of those offenses. But however

big they were, however vivid the details, no matter how much
pain was there, the person who most needed my forgiveness was
none other than myself. I had to start with me. For years, I had
been obsessed with my flaws, my weaknesses, and the self-imposed limits that made life seem doable instead of worth doing.
I had yet to understand that my value was inherent and came
from God. Genuine love is unconditional, and I had given myself countless parameters. For as long as I could remember, I
lived within the confines of a multitude of self-imposed rules.
I guess I figured if I didn't comply, I would end up like one of
those hapless people I wanted to help, not really getting it that
I already was — however imperceptible it may have seemed on
the outside.

Many of us need to forgive ourselves as much as our neighbor. We're disappointed in the way our lives have turned out. We
feel lingering guilt about something we've done and don't think
we are worthy of forgiveness. Even after confession we sometimes feel unable to accept the mercy of redemption. C. S. Lewis
pointed out, "If God forgives us, we must forgive ourselves. Oth-
erwise, it is almost like setting up ourselves as a higher tribunal
than him." Holding on to grievances not only hurts you, it hurts
God. He made the ultimate sacrifice for you, and while that may
not make forgiving your neighbor any easier, it does make it necessary. Your salvation is made possible through forgiveness and
hinges on your willingness to forgive. It's easy to be distracted by
the rules of religion, the rituals, the multitude of ways in which
we sin, all of which have a place in your spiritual life. But what
is paramount is God's genuine, infinite, sacrificial, and unconditional love.

I needed forgiveness so I could live in the fullness that God
wants for my life. The world offers many ways to save ourselves
through self-reliance, self-awareness, and self-care, but God offers only one: *forgiveness*. Having a full life isn't about your ré-

sumé or any other quantifiable way that society measures your worth. The most beautiful part of our faith is what came out of the brutal crucifixion of our Savior. Don't let that be for naught. It was for you and for me — for all of us. Forgive yourself and rejoice in the resurrection waiting for you.

TURN THE OTHER CHEEK

I met an atheist through a mutual friend and was speaking to him about God when he asked, "Where was God today then, when that baby got shot and killed on his walk?" He proceeded to tell me about a robbery attempt involving a one-year-old being shot in his stroller while out on a walk with his mother. Obviously, this was unimaginable and horrific. When I went home and listened as the baby's father was interviewed on the news, he had just come back from saying goodbye to his dead son. While he said that the gunman and his companion must be punished, he offered forgiveness for what they did. He said he would pray for them.

Only through the grace of God could a father have the strength to forgive the murder of his innocent baby and to offer the gift of prayer for the perpetrator. It's a remarkable example of someone turning to God in darkness instead of away from

> *"Do not rejoice over me, O my enemy; / when I fall, I shall rise."*
> *(Micah 7:8)*

him. That father imitated God's mercy at a time when it was hardly plausible to believe forgiveness is possible. Only through God could this be.

Although many of us find it difficult, most of us understand the need for forgiveness. Saint Francis of Paola explains it with poignant clarity: "Remembering grievances works great damage. It is accompanied by anger, fosters sin, and brings a hatred for justice. It is a rusty arrow spreading poison in the soul. It destroys virtue and is a cancer in the mind. It thwarts prayer and mangles the petitions we make to God. It drives out love and is a nail driven into the soul, an evil that never sleeps, a sin that never fades away, a kind of daily death." While we may desire resurrection from such a death, knowing how to forgive can feel as overwhelming and impossible as putting together a 5,000-piece puzzle. We have no clue how to make the mountain of pieces whole. We can't find the corner pieces in the mess or figure out where to start. But perhaps forgiveness has nothing to do with putting back together the mosaic of what has broken us. Instead, maybe it's letting it go, piece by piece. Replace the piece that tells us it's impossible by knowing all things are possible with God. Exchange the piece that plays our grievances like a warbled record over and over for the quiet of God's peace. Swap the piece that says "they" don't deserve our forgiveness for God's merciful healing. Leave all those pieces that burden, imprison, and distract you at the foot of the cross.

We don't have to put back together our heartbreak — we can leave it with Jesus.

REDEMPTION SONG

The last day of vacation I woke up with a tingling feeling on my lips. When I looked in the mirror, even through the blur of the dim morning light I could tell my lips were noticeably fuller — like the fairy godmother of plastic surgery had visited in the night. My pink pout was the result of a sunburn from a long day of scalloping with friends and family. I cringed thinking of the resulting sun damage and started down the long, twisty road of lament and regret I know so well. Then, for the love of mercy, I had a thought that framed itself as a question in the highlight reel of my mind: *Why would you ever think you would get through life unscathed?* Life is full of losses. We lose money. We lose jobs. We lose time. We lose things that are dear to us. We lose people we love. *We lose.* No one likes to lose, either. We live in a world that tells us life is all about the win. We are encouraged to minimize cost and maximize gains. While that makes good sense in a lot of sunny scenarios, the reality is, sunburn or not, none of us gets through life without experiencing a burn. Accepting this as part of our humanity somehow dulls the sting of it. Perhaps so much of our suffering is exacerbated by our resistance to it and our refusal to forgive the source of our loss.

> *"For God so loved the world that he gave his only Son, so that everyone who believes in him may not perish but may have eternal life."*
>
> *(John 3:16)*

Resentment and sin weigh us down. Forgiveness allows us to unload the burden of sin. It's the mercy of a do-over. Sometimes forgiving others feels empowering. Other times, "Seventy times seven" just feels hard (cf. Mt 18:22).

Yet at the end of our lives, we will encounter Easter. In between, in the thicket of life's trespasses, we rise. No matter how difficult, we are called to rise to the mercy of forgiveness. Jesus did the impossible. He did the miraculous. He transformed death. Thus, our suffering does not have to define us. Our injuries do not have to bind us. Challenge, adversity, and wounds do not have to stop our ascent. We rise when we ask for forgiveness. We rise when we forgive others. Despite our brokenness, the shedding of our burdens, the surrendering of our bitterness at the foot of his cross, and the unification of our souls to his, makes our rising possible.

MERCY WORKS: TRY IT

"He is the atoning sacrifice for our sins, and not for ours only but also for the sins of the whole world" (1 Jn 2:2). Let's imitate this profound mercy by forgiving others.

- *In your home*: Say sorry. Teach your children how to make a good apology. Don't say "but" during an apology ("I am sorry I hurt you, *but* ..."). Practice forgiveness with small things. Especially in marriage, forgiveness is important. When you hurt your spouse, ask for forgiveness. When someone makes a mistake, be gracious. Remind children that we all make mistakes and that accidents happen. Encourage family members to share their grievances. It's healthy to tell someone you feel hurt by something they said or did. Explain the importance of talking about pain, giving wounds air so they can heal instead of pushing them down where they fester. After acknowledging frustrations or hurts, let them go. Don't bring them up again. Don't say "you always" or "you never." Instead try, "Okay, I understand" or "I know you didn't mean to intentionally hurt me." If you are having trouble forgiving something, ask God for the grace to help you. He will.

- *In your community*: Practice an attitude of forgiveness. Don't sweat the small stuff. When you encounter friends and coworkers who vent to you about grievances, encourage forgiveness. Act as a facilitator of mercy. Remind them of our humanness and our call to forgive. Be compassionate about their pain, but don't prolong it by emphasizing the perpetrator's flaws or mistake. Consider volunteering with a prison ministry or a group that helps newly released prisoners reacclimate to society. Sign petitions against the death penalty and protest its use. Volunteer with at-risk juveniles and mentor them on the path of redemption. Model Jesus' example and bestow mercy and forgiveness lavishly.

- *In your personal relationship with God:* Go to confession often. Say the Act of Contrition or pray the Chaplet of Divine Mercy daily. It is the most incredible gift to be forgiven. God wants to forgive us; he's just waiting for us to ask. So ask him for forgiveness. Thank him for his mercy. Study parables in the Bible about forgiveness, like the Parable of the Two Debtors and the Prodigal Son. Read stories of others' redemption for inspiration and encouragement. Leave whatever grudges burden you at the foot of the cross. Walk away from grudges and into the light of redemption. You can do it. He will help you. Let him.

REFLECTION QUESTIONS

Whom do you need to forgive?

How has being forgiven by others changed you or a situation?

How does receiving forgiveness in the Sacrament of Reconciliation help motivate you to let go of grievances towards others?

PRAYER

Dear Heavenly Father, I am ashamed of the ways I have hurt you and others. I hate the ways my failings have separated me from you. I ask you to wash away the pain of my wounds and the burdens of my sin. Free me from resentments, grudges, and the grief of holding on to what you have commanded that I set free. Give me the strength to avoid sin, the resolve to forgive others, and the joy of resurrection that your forgiveness has made possible. Let me never forget the reason for the wounds of the cross, nor let me add to them through my own iniquities. In your most merciful name, I pray.

14

Pray for the Living and the Dead

"Call to me and I will answer you, and will tell you great and hidden things that you have not known."

Jeremiah 33:3

While Teresa was being rushed to the hospital for complications from the flu, I prayed the Rosary. The memory is like a blur — head racing, rosary beads twisting, stomach clenching, hands shaking, and heart aching. I was anxious to get to the emergency room, but a voice from somewhere inside repeated: *Pray. Pray. Pray.* When I finished the Rosary, I got on Facebook and implored others to pray, too. I begged, "even if you don't pray — *pray anyway.*" I'm not usually bossy on social media, so I hoped the urgency of my appeal would be understood. Even if it wasn't their friend or situation, even if they were estranged from God, I needed prayers for my friend. I figured if someone lacked faith, they could borrow their neighbor's and toss something up to God. He's a great catcher. That's what he does over and over — he catches us. He doesn't get caught up in who knows whom, or the grudges someone is holding against him. He isn't keeping score. He just catches.

Within hours, Teresa died. My prayers were different then. Praying for the dead is specific in the Catholic Faith. It begins at the moment of death as a way to both honor and atone for the deceased, and it doesn't end with the funeral Mass. It's an ongoing way to ensure that the heavenly promise of our faith is fulfilled for the departed. "From the beginning the Church has honored the memory of the dead and offers prayers in suffrage for them, above all the Eucharistic sacrifice, so that, thus purified, they may attain the beatific vision of God" (CCC 1032). After Teresa's death, my prayers were a culmination of joy for the years we shared. They were of gratitude for our friendship that even the razor-sharp pain of grief could not dull. Strangely, they were also of peace, of quiet that was not empty, and of a knowing that in the descent of death, God caught her.

He caught me that day, too. He has been holding me up ever since, reminding me that the power of prayer isn't in how it's answered. It's in the strength that comes from the love in which it's offered. Through a litany of prayer, love enveloped my friend on the day she died and all the days since. By remembering that we are members of the same Communion of Saints, I don't feel so separate from her, despite her death. Through that union, I pray that she is rejoicing with God in heaven, and I trust that she is watching over and interceding for all of us. In that way our friendship lives on. It's become its own kind of prayer.

This work of mercy is about interceding on behalf of the living and the dead through prayer. When God sees us coming to him to petition for the needs of our neighbor, he is moved by our love. Interceding for others expands our own hearts and attunes us to God's mercy. As part of the Communion of Saints, we are called to intercede for one another. According to the *Catechism of the Catholic Church*, "We believe in the communion of all the faithful of Christ, those who are pilgrims on earth, the dead who are being purified, and the blessed in heaven, all together forming one church; and we believe that in this communion, the merciful love of God and his saints is always attentive to our prayers" (CCC, 962). In the Communion of Saints, we have the unceasing intercession of our guardian angels and saints; of Mary, our gentle mother who goes straight from our hearts to the heart of Jesus; of the Holy Spirit as our advocate; and of Jesus Christ as our mediator and Redeemer. We also have the unity of the faithful, both living and dead. No wonder people say there is power in prayer. In the Communion of Saints, we have an army of love warriors who seek to bring peace to our hearts and to those for whom we pray.

> *"Again, truly I tell you, if two of you agree on earth about anything you ask, it will be done for you by my Father in heaven."*
>
> *(Matthew 18:19)*

ASK

At a routine eye exam, I was surprised when the optometrist

called in another doctor to take a look at my son Alex's eyes. The doctor had already commented on his perfect vision. I listened to them consult in some kind of code language that made my stomach tighten and breath slow. Finally, the optometrist explained that something was pressing into his eye. My seven-year-old would need an MRI. Both boys were in the room and oblivious that the conversation had turned to tumors.

I've always been happy to pray for the intentions of others. However, when it came to asking for prayers for Alex, I felt strangely paralyzed. Instead of reaching out to those I knew who could intercede for me, I initially went inward. As a member of a prayer group that prays for the school's students and our own children, I sat tensely at our weekly meeting. I swore to myself I wasn't going to share Alex's situation with the group. It was my cross. I was determined to carry it alone. It's hard to know if the words came first or the sobs. But all at once it was out: the eye exam, the frustration of dealing with doctors, the potential brain tumor, the fear, and the gut-wrenching horror of it all. And those beautiful ladies prayed *with* me. The distinction between praying *with* someone or *for* someone may not always be obvious, but sitting in the shelter of that small group, having them unite their petitions to mine, was incredibly meaningful. They helped lift my cross for a moment of merciful relief. I realized I wasn't alone and that, regardless of the outcome, there was a faith community ready and willing to see me through.

Ultimately, Alex did not have a tumor. A brain surgeon explained the misshapen brain that the MRI revealed was just an anomaly. His brain was unique, not cancerous. Needing prayers from others isn't unique either. We should never feel hesitant to ask for them. Even if it's uncomfortable, praying with someone else is a profound mercy. Trusting others with our sacred prayer intentions draws us closer and strengthens the community of saints to which we belong. God wants us to lift each other in prayer. Whether it's praying for the world, the Church, the departed, the souls in purgatory, those you dislike, or those who can't pray for themselves, prayer unites us in a way that is timeless and for all time.

> *"So I tell you, whatever you ask for in prayer, believe that you have received it, and it will be yours." (Mark 11:24)*

BELIEVE AND RECEIVE

During one Christmas season, I was reminded of the power of prayer when I became one of the prayer warriors trying to get a forty-nine-year-old man named Joe out of prison. I know that doesn't conjure the same feelings of drinking hot cocoa in footed pajamas by the fire like your typical Christmas story does. Still, it's a powerful reminder of what can happen when we believe — not only in God but in one another.

As one of six boys, Joe grew up next door to my friend, Cecy. Despite having three young kids at home, she worked for years trying to get her childhood friend out of prison. Joe had been arrested for buying cocaine for personal use and was charged and sentenced as a trafficker. His punishment was twenty years with no chance of parole. He had already served thirteen.

Joe had made appeals all the way to the Florida Supreme Court — each one denied. The only hope he had was clemency from the governor to commute his sentence. That's when the ordinary became extraordinary. Joe was finally granted a clemency hearing. Sadly, his mom passed away less than a month before his hearing. Joe learned of her death from a prison guard and was unable to attend her funeral. The tragedy of it hardly made

188 *The Spiritual Works of Mercy*

me think of the word, *believe*. Yet when his hearing was finally held, I was visiting New York City where over the Macy's store on 34th Street, a huge sign in brilliant white lights said only one word: *Believe*. While I wasn't sure whether I believed our prayers would be answered in the way that we wanted, I was inspired by the people who believed Joe deserved another chance and did something about it. I had faith that no matter what, God would use the situation for good. I had already seen how many people it had united in prayer and I felt the shared hope that a miracle was possible. *I very much wanted to believe.*

"Rejoice in hope, be patient in suffering, persevere in prayer."

(Romans 12:12)

On the morning of his clemency hearing, I received a text from Cecy with the novena prayer we had been praying to Our Lady of Guadalupe. Serendipitously, his hearing fell on the feast day of Our Lady of Guadalupe, and it was the last day of our novena. I knew his chances were slim. This governor had never commuted a sentence before. Feeling anxious, I intermittently listened to the hearing in our hotel room. Joe's good friend told the clemency board and the governor about how he and his children visited Joe in prison. He spoke of the time his daughter was asked to choose the Catholic she admired most, and she chose Joe. One of Joe's brothers read a letter from Joe, who accepted responsibility for his crime. He asked for mercy.

My eyes pooled when Cecy's eighty-year-old mother spoke — after her eight-hour commute to the Florida State Capitol Building — about the little boy of her best friend of forty years. She said Joe was a good man who gave in to the temptation of drugs. She testified that indeed he had a strong network of friends and family who would support his transition out of prison, but that his mother has a greater network of friends in heaven who would make sure he stays on the right path.

The last speaker on Joe's behalf said, "As I understand it, clemency is mercy or favor or grace, and a relief from a just penalty. I am reminded of that definition during Advent, as we approach the commemoration of the birth of Christ." I thought about the birth of the baby in the manger and all the generations of believers who have brought petitions, pleas, and requests for pardon before Jesus since that momentous night in the stable. Our prayers that day were just one in the flurry of billions he had heard. *But God heard.* The governor did what he had never done before. He granted clemency. Joe would be given a second chance, just in time for Christmas. Besotted with gratitude, I went to St. Patrick's Cathedral and lit a candle at the altar dedicated to Our Lady of Guadalupe, which was covered in flowers and surrounded by people who had come to honor her feast day.

It's easy to stop believing. One day you realize there is no Santa Claus. There are no talking snowmen, elves, or flying reindeer. That magic is gone, and we think it is okay because it's childish and silly and there is no room for that in our grown-up, real-world lives. But our Christian faith is no fairy tale. It requires us to keep believing in the power of prayer, the Communion of Saints, and the mercy of intercession. Having faith that people will stand by you at your darkest hour, petition, forgive, and believe you are worth a second try, reminds us what it means to emulate the life of Christ. Those are the people who inspire us to *believe.*

WAIT

Rushing to get somewhere, I was stopped by a red light — *a very long red light.* My heart pumping, brain whizzing, my hands gripping the steering wheel, I felt certain the world would end if the stoplight didn't turn green that instant. As cars whizzed by, I watched enviously, wondering when it would be my turn, wondering if the light was broken, wondering how much longer I could possibly wait as all of humankind seemingly passed by at an unimpressive forty miles per hour. That's what it feels like with prayer sometimes — an agonizing, monotonous wait. While we know God's timing is not our own, there are still moments in our prayer lives where we feel the same urgency as I did at that stoplight. "Ask, and it will be given to you; search, and you will find; knock, and the door will be opened for you" (Mt 7:7). Stop at a red light and it will turn green. *Presto.* Prayer answered. It seems that Scripture should come with a bible-sized addendum outlining exceptions, exclusions, and caveats to explain the time gap between asking and receiving. Sometimes the wait for an answered prayer feels like an eternity.

As frustrating as waiting can be, it's also when we can be the most faithful. Waiting for God to answer prayers requires patience, trust, and faithfulness to his will. *It's hard.* We don't know how long it will be before we get an answer. We aren't guaranteed the answer we want. We get annoyed when Garth Brooks sings about unanswered prayers. Still, it's at this crossroad when we decide if we are going to be faithful to God. By developing a strong personal habit of prayer and committing to listening to God's will, we have the necessary tools to endure what can feel impossible. Prayer gets us where we need to go — in an entirely different kind of light.

REJOICE

At the center of my computer is an icon of a light bulb that reads, "Tell me what you want to do." Maybe it's because I had a perpetually messy room as a child and watched too many episodes of *I Dream of Jeannie*, but I've been looking for a light bulb like that my entire life. Haven't we all? How much simpler life would be if we could just get what we want, what we think we need, what we know will finally fill that persistent ache of our humanity.

Growing up, I didn't consider how hard life could be. I didn't think about cancer, or addiction, miscarriages or infertility, suicide or loneliness. I just saw an empty stage with endless possibilities. Plenty of time for laughter, love, and happy endings. As naïve as it may seem, I wish I still believed this — that time and possibilities are infinite. Instead, what I *know* is more precious: Life is fleeting, like the blink of a firefly on a summer night. It sparkles and dances and sometimes burns out too quickly. It's a chance to spread love, make things better, and embrace gratitude as our truest friend. It can be gritty and gruesome and flat-out heartbreak-

"Do not worry about anything, but in everything by prayer and supplication with thanksgiving let your requests be made known to God. And the peace of God, which surpasses all understanding, will guard your hearts and your minds in Christ Jesus."

(Philippians 4:6–7)

ing. Life isn't a "your wish is my command" experience, but it is magical, even if that magic feels black at times. I've learned every stage has challenges, triumphs, and part of the answer of what God calls us to do. The sufferings I lamented, resented, and mourned have shaped me into a wiser, stronger, and more resilient person. They've also taught me to surrender, be softer, and stand firm.

I bring the waves of vacillation that shape my life to the altar during the Eucharist as a plea: *Tell me what you want me to do, God.* It is the ultimate prayer. I feel more connected to him at this moment than any other. I feel both surrender and strength. Sometimes it feels scary, like a dare. *Will I do what he asks? Will I obey?* Other times, it feels like a brave truth. I trust in his mercy, have faith in his plan, and feel such genuine love that I know it will bridge the difference between truth and dare. Prayer has evolved from being a means to get what I want to a way to give what he wills. The trajectory of life, with all the roads that sometimes felt too narrow, too fast, too winding, and too dark, led to him. It's not as simple as the light bulb icon on the computer screen promises, but it illuminates the darkest parts of life. Not by giving in to our demands, but by reminding us to rejoice in his commandment of love — a prayer that leads to everlasting life.

MERCY WORKS: TRY IT

"Pray without ceasing" (1 Thes 5:17). Let us unite our hearts to God's and live our lives as a prayer, always keeping in mind the needs of our neighbors and our intercessory prayers for the deceased.

- *In your home*: Pray as a family. You might pray the Rosary, novenas, and specific prayers for one another's special intentions. Attend Eucharistic adoration together. Keep a prayer list for family members' special intentions. Remember death anniversaries of those close to your family and create special prayer rituals to intercede for them. Teach your children to pray for people who hurt others, for the lonely, and for those who don't have a relationship with God. Encourage involvement in youth groups and conferences. Set aside a certain time each day to pray outwardly with your spouse. Remind your children of God's presence in nature and how God speaks to us through creation. Do a family Bible study together and use the seasons of Advent and Lent as opportunities to strengthen and lengthen your prayer life.

- *In your community*: Pray randomly for the person you drive by during your commute, the cashier ringing you up, and the person you passed walking the dog. Pray publicly in front of your church, children's school, or an abortion clinic. Start a prayer or Rosary group and invite others. Pray for the people you read about on the news, our public and Church leaders, and the forgotten. Find a prayer partner who will share intentions with you, pray with you, and work to hold each other accountable. Pray for the dead — those you love and those you never knew. Attend funerals and remember the deceased during prayers at Mass. Serve others as a prayer making the connection between deed and deity.

- *In your personal relationship with God*: Make prayer an organic part of your daily life, weaving it into morning, afternoon, and evening rituals. Keep a prayer journal and write letters to God. Spend quiet time in prayer. Attend adoration, weekday Mass, and holy hours. Pray the Rosary daily. Attend religious retreats and conferences as often as possible.

Seek opportunities and ways to pray for others, living and dead.

REFLECTION QUESTIONS

What are some ways God might be inviting you to have more patience or trust as you wait for the answer to a prayer?

Does praying to a saint or praying the Rosary feel different to you than when you talk straight to God? Which are you more drawn to and why?

How can you make others feel more comfortable about asking for prayer intentions or allowing you to pray with them?

PRAYER

Dear Heavenly Father, help me draw closer to you through prayer. Help my actions align with my heart so that my service is an expression of my deepest love for you. May your holy name be always on my lips and may my life be a witness to your inexhaustible mercy and love. Make me available to the prayer needs of others so that I can intercede for them. Help me to remember the most vulnerable in my prayers, and during difficult times of life help me unite my suffering to yours through unceasing prayer.

Afterword

"Keep alert, stand firm in your faith, be courageous,
be strong. Let all that you do be done in love."
1 Corinthians 16:13–14

The popular book *The Elf on the Shelf: A Christmas Tradition* became a household sensation for parents of young children. As the story goes, elves hide in homes during the day and then fly back to the North Pole at night to tell Santa Claus if children were naughty or nice. Each morning the elf hides in a new place. Of course, the world being what it is, this quickly evolved into parents completing complicated and intricate elf activities every single night of the already exhausting holiday season. It was no longer enough for the elf to move to a new place. Now, elves were getting their own outfits; sleds made out of graham crackers, icing, and peppermints; clever messages tediously written in tiny red and green candies; and elf sack races and scrabble games.

A friend told me how her young daughter would come home from school and report on all of the wacky, fun antics her classmates' elves did the night before. Her daughter was disappointed in their obviously slacker elf who only moved around the house, instead of painstakingly crafting a marshmallow igloo featuring a candied fireplace where a tiny elf stocking lovingly hung above the edible fire. One night my friend found a note her daughter left for their elf. It simply read: *Do more.*

More is the directive of the day. As absurd as this may seem when thinking about the clever tricks of spying elves, it's indicative of how the command of more has seeped into almost every facet of modern life. Every day in countless ways, the world communicates that we need to do more to measure up or even just keep up. Meanwhile, I often feel like the amiable comic book character Pig Pen, created by Charles Shultz, traveling in my own dust storm with all the to-do's swirling around making a filthy mess of what could be a peaceful mind. No matter what I did, it never felt like enough and the dirt caked on — further muddying my panic of more.

The problem with more is that it inevitably makes us feel like *less*. It challenges the truth of our inherent value as children of God. It destroys our sense of self-worth and diminishes the quality of our relationships. It makes service feel like another chore instead of a way to connect to God, who doesn't need us to prove anything. There are always so many things we are being asked to do, change, and improve about ourselves. Yet so much of what is suggested is superficial, temporary, and unfulfilling.

What the world really needs more of is *mercy.*

The works of mercy aren't just another gimmick. They are game-changers. When I tried these works of mercy as an alternative to the creed of the secular world, I found less striving, less busying, less dissatisfaction, less emptiness, and more time for my relationship with God, my family, and the people I love. I found more meaning, more compassion, and more clarity than I'd ever found in anything the world offered.

Mostly, through mercy I found myself. I laid all of my brokenness at the foot of the cross and walked away finally feeling like I was *enough*. This is my hope for you — that you, too, will make a deliberate decision to reevaluate your life and service through the lens of mercy. You may be surprised at how much you finally like what you see. By saturating our lives in God's inexhaustible mercy, our collective compassion can change the world. Life might always be as messy as Pig Pen, but mercy reminds us that Pig Pen always carried himself with dignity despite the dirt that squiggled around him. He even proudly referred to it as "the dust of ancient civilizations." We too can carry ourselves with the dignity of Christ despite how disheveled the world may be. Life might always be messy, but God's mercy and the love we show for our neighbor is the light that shines through the dust — revealing the dawn of a new day.

May it be more than you ever hoped for.

About the Author

Lara C. Patangan is a freelance writer whose writing appears on CatholicMom.com, Blessed Is She, *Our Sunday Visitor*, and *St. Augustine Catholic*. In lieu of a more regrettable midlife crisis, she spent her fortieth year doing corporal and spiritual works of mercy. Along the way, she discovered some remarkable things about the openhearted generosity of others and the power of simple mercies to change lives. More than anything, she realized her own hungry need for mercy. Knowing God through his mercy has been one of the saving graces of her life, and she firmly believes that no act of kindness is ordinary or insignificant. A wife and mother of two boys, she considers her family her greatest mercy, for they are more than she could have ever hoped for. Please visit her website, larapatangan.com, to join a community that believes in the power of mercy to change the world.